THE PRACTICE CO

*Devotions and reflections for thoughtful spirituality
by Liz Milani*

VOLUME 02

WELCOME

Hey, friend! I'm Liz, in case we haven't met yet. Welcome to Volume Two of the book version of The Practice Co. Rumi said, "*The rewards of life and devotion to God are love and inner rapture, and the capacity to receive the light of God.*" The Practice Co is a place for us to explore this devotion... not just read a devotional, but to practice a devoted life centred around the integration of the human and the holy; the ordinary and the divine. For too long, faith has been about getting us out of our bodies, but I believe that's exactly where God wants us: content in our own skin, embodied and paying attention. It's my intention that these series of devotionals and reflections will wake you up to the divinity within you and around you, and will compel you to fall in love with your own life all over again as you find The Divine right in the middle of it all.

You can binge them, savour them one at a time, work your way through with pens and highlighters and scribbles on the page... whatever works for you is what you should do. And listen, these are not rules or stipulations or must do's or even exactly the way things are. Each theme and line and premise is a suggestion, a starting point, the first step in a journey of many. Let them ignite your imagination and faith and set you on course to find out for yourself what it is you believe and want and will practice. My motto these days is: take what's helpful, leave the rest. And enjoy. Have fun. Play. As you do, I pray that on this journey of devotion, you find love, inner rapture, and the capacity to receive the Light of God.

FIND OUT MORE:

Check out our Daily Devotional App for iOS and Android at **thepracticeco.com/app**

Follow us on Instagram: **@thepracticeco**

Website: **thepracticeco.com**

TABLE OF CONTENTS

- **2** — DEVOTION
  What does a life of devotion look like?

- **16** — GET YOUR FIGHT BACK
  When to fight? When to surrender?

- **34** — NOTE TO SELF
  What messages do you send yourself?

- **50** — ROOM FOR MYSTERY
  Finding peace beyond certainty.

- **68** — THE GOOD DARK
  Transformation in the dark.

- **80** — WHO DO YOU THINK YOU ARE?
  Overcoming Imposter Syndrome.

- **96** — DROP YOUR NETS
  Recognising your life changing moment.

- **110** — THE WAY BACK
  How do you find the way back to you? To peace? To wonder? To childlike faith?

"INSTRUCTIONS FOR LIVING A LIFE. PAY ATTENTION. BE ASTONISHED. TELL ABOUT IT."

Mary Oliver

DEVOTION - PART 1
Paying Attention

How's your devotional practice?

What does it look like?

What did you think of when I asked that question?

When you do a Google search, or better yet, Pinterest search, for devotion, it's incredible what you find. The results are blog posts and images mostly outlining the top ten ways to have a successful quiet time, or the seven essential elements to prayer and bible reading, or the three things you must do if you're serious about living a life devoted to God. And all of them? They're about what you do within a thirty-minute window at least once a day. If you want tips on how to read the Bible better and how to pray properly when 'x,' 'y,' or 'z' is happening in your life, then friend, Google is for you.

The word devotion has been reduced to a function, a chore, an activity to be ticked off the "How to be a good Christian" list. It has become something defined and scalable, something you can fit into a box. And look, it's not lost on me that what I do here at The Practice Co is filed under the category of 'devotional.' But to be honest, I've never been comfortable calling my writing 'devotions,' not in the traditional sense of the word. I don't want anyone to think we're suggesting that reading a few paragraphs a day will lead them into 'all and absolute' truth.

I grew up in a small Pentecostal church in the countryside of New South Wales, Australia, where daily devotionals were little snippets of scripture and explanations on how to live right and holy and pleasing to God. The devotionals I devoured rarely allowed room for my questions or the greyness I held in my heart and that I saw in the world around me. I barely lived up to them either; I was always falling short of the lesson and striving to do better, be better... everything better.

But you don't read truth, you live into it. The Biblical text can't be explained in a few short paragraphs or definitively explained at all. Devotion is not about how you fill a window of time with prayer and bible reading, then check it off on your list of 'Good Christian Behaviour.'

Devotion is a way of life.

"PAYING ATTENTION IS THE BEGINNING OF DEVOTION" — *Mary Oliver*

Devotion is a commitment to living in such a way that keeps us awake, aware and alive to Divine Presence. A devotional life is not one with hip and cool tips and tricks about how to read your bible and pray better, but one that has learned the unforced rhythms of grace that live into truth, questions, and faith alike. Being a person of faith isn't about following a set of rules, it's a way of living your life open and full: devoted and paying attention.

The word devotion simply means loyalty motived by love. In Ancient Hebrew, no word translates exactly into devotion... the closest thing to it is the word Chesed, which means loving kindness. This was the word used to express the original concept of grace. Grace is a creative force — an act of exceptional kindness and goodness that never ceases to expand and include and grow.

Loyalty, love, grace, and kindness: four things that will open your heart, cause you to pay attention, and bring you to the middle and meat of life.

Instead of asking, "How is your devotional practice," we should ask, "How much do you love? Are you paying attention? Can you see beauty?"

Every prayer we pray, every post we read, every verse we contemplate, should lead us to the place of falling in love and opening our hearts to wonder, grace, and growth.

DEVOTION - PART 2
Loyal to Love

"In the deepest sense love is not something you do. It is something you become—a loving person."
—Dallas Willard

The word devotion means "loyalty motivated by love." It is not the function of reading your bible and praying for however many minutes a day; it is not your 'quiet time with Jesus,' and it is not something you can tick off a list once you've completed the task. Devotion never ceases.

To discover devotion, we have to figure out what loyalty is. So, what is it? What are you loyal to? And what does that look like?

Most modern ideas of devotion have us being loyal to form and function: reading/journaling/praying. Which, of course, you can reduce 'devotion' to being loyal and in love with an idea or an activity within which we seek to understand a subject. But God is not an idea or a subject. God is not a fact to be grasped or an idea to comprehend.

St Augustine said: *"If you have understood, then what you have understood is not God."*

God cannot be understood as much as God can be experienced. In a series of talks called "The Power of Paradox," Father Rohr said:

"Many mystics speak of the God-experience as simultaneously falling into an abyss and being grounded. This sounds like a contradiction, but in fact, when you allow yourself to fall into the abyss—into hiddenness, limitlessness, unknowability, a void without boundaries—you discover it's somehow a rich, supportive, embracing spaciousness where you don't have to ask (or answer) the questions of whether you're right or wrong. You're being held and so you do not need to try to "hold" yourself together... Mystery is not something you can't know. Mystery is endless knowability. Living inside such endless knowability is finally a comfort, a foundation of ultimate support, security, unrestricted love, and eternal care."

The Ancient Hebrew word for loyalty is Chesed, which is also the Ancient Hebrew word for loving kindness from which the original concept of grace flows. Our Hebrew mothers and fathers believed that it was with and for Chesed - loyalty, grace, love, and kindness - that God created the cosmos. God who is good created so God could be involved in collective goodness so that God could be good to and within that which God created.

"Your love, God, is my song, and I'll sing it! I'm forever telling everyone how faithful you are. I'll never quit telling the story of your love—how you built the cosmos and guaranteed everything in it. Your love has always been our lives' foundation, your fidelity has been the roof over our world." Ps 89:3 (MSG).

Have you ever questioned God's loyalty?

I have.

I've cried and prayed and screamed and shouted. I've questioned and doubted and waited in silence and stormed off in anger. And I'm not alone. The Psalms gave language to my angst, as have many theologians and authors and Spiritual leaders.

Where are you God? Where is your loyalty? Why haven't you intervened?

On a podcast I heard recently, Anne Lamott said that "if I was God's east coast rep, I would be doing things a lot different than what God's current rep was doing."

But loyalty isn't devotion to form or function or activity. It's more personal than that, more human than that, more mysterious - endlessly knowable - than that.

It is not disloyal to question, or to doubt, or to seek. It is not disloyal if you can't do what someone expects you too, or even what they need you to do. The highest act of disloyalty is to stop paying attention.

And in that, we are disloyal creatures hoping that the gracious aspect of Chesed will carry us across the line. Which, if we stay open and humble and attentive, it always does.

The Divine may not check off all the 'To Do's' on our list of what we think God needs to achieve, but The Divine never stops paying attention.

There's a deeper loyalty in question here:

What if we were loyal to love? What if we were loyal to grace? Mercy? Kindness? And justice? Even for ourselves?

DEVOTION - PART 3
Something You Become

Are you devoted to form? Or are you devoted to being?

When you're devoted to the form of something, the ritual becomes the God, the thing that is worshiped, revered, and idealised. It's like being in love with love...
you're not in love with a person, but in the idea of being in love. You fantasise about what being in love would be like, because the object of your affection is not the person you love, but the idea of being in love. And in this state of being in love with love, you just

might miss love when it's right beneath your nose.

Many idealise and worship their devotional practice, more than the object of the practice itself. The reading and the praying and the listing and the timing become the goal, rather than connection and presence and wonder and engagement.

Sometimes our devotion gets in the way of our devotion.

In Acts chapter ten, a man named Peter fell into a deep trance. The Greek word used for trance is the word for ecstasy. So whatever Peter is experiencing, we can assume it's not your every day ordinary plain-flavoured vision. While in this trance, Peter experienced some crazy stuff. He saw heaven open, and from the open sky dropped a sheet full of animals - reptiles, birds, and mammals. And as the sheet full of swarming animals settled on the ground, a voice called to Peter: Get up, kill, and eat.

Something you need to know about Peter: he grew up in Capernaum, a fishing village that was known for its fierce commitment to Torah. This commitment to the Hebrew Bible and the Commandments included the laws around purity which were all about how to stay clean, and how to avoid becoming unclean. Which included laws about what you could eat, who you could eat with, how you killed what you ate, and who you hung around with. Just like touching a dead animal you found on the side of the road, or eating pork made you unclean, so did touching or eating with someone who was considered unclean. Their devotion to purity was so extreme, they wouldn't even consider going into the house of someone thought to be unclean, which was basically anyone who wasn't Jewish.

So when an otherworldly voice boomed down from heaven and told Peter to get up, kill whatever he wanted, and eat it, Peter replied:

"There's no way I could do that, Lord, for I've never eaten anything forbidden or impure according to our Jewish laws."

The voice spoke again.

"Nothing is unclean if God declares it to be clean."

The vision was repeated three times. Then suddenly the linen sheet was snatched back up into heaven. Peter was so stunned by the vision that he couldn't stop wondering about what all it meant. (Acts 10:14-17.)

God told Peter that he could eat whatever he wanted, but Peter told God that he couldn't possibly do that because he was so devoted to Torah, and had been all his life, he couldn't break his devotion to it. Essentially, Peter defied God in the name of God.

The form and the function had become the idol.

Now, Chesed - loyalty, grace, loving-kindness - is a generative, creative force. It's how and why The Divine created the cosmos, from the heavens to our cells, and its why and how the earth is still generating, creating, expanding, becoming... Healthy devotion always leads to growth, it never stagnates.

Form is static, presence is dynamic.

When you're devoted to the function of something, including your faith, you miss the dance that the form is inviting you into, just as Peter was about to find out. Because as soon as his trance lifted, there was a knock at his door...

He was about to discover that:

"IN THE DEEPEST SENSE LOVE IS NOT SOMETHING YOU DO. IT IS SOMETHING YOU BECOME—A LOVING PERSON." — *Dallas Willard*

DEVOTION - PART 4
A Life of Faith

One day, when Peter was hungry, he fell into a trance - a moment of ecstasy, as the Greek suggests. While in this trance, he saw the skies open, a sheet full of four-footed animals, reptiles and wild birds fall from the sky and land before him and heard a voice say "Get up. Kill. Eat."

But Peter protested. He had seriously and consistently kept all the purity laws according to his religion and wasn't about to change his ways. He told the voice (whom he called Lord) that he couldn't and wouldn't.

The voice said back to him:

"Nothing is unclean if God declares it to be clean." (Acts 10:15 TPT.)

I wonder how many things and people and ideas and communities God has declared clean that we still will not touch because we're devoted to the structure and form of something, rather than the essence it always intended to reveal?

The story continues that while Peter was trying to make sense of what he saw while entranced, three Roman men knocked on his door and said that they needed Peter to come with them to the house of a Roman official to speak with him.

Now, remember, Peter had just told the voice in his vision that he had no intention of defiling the purity laws. These purity laws were about food AND people. Just as eating something deemed unclean made you so, so did going into the house or eating a meal or associating with someone who wasn't of the Jewish faith.

Something was happening inside Peter. His devotion to form was being challenged. He left his house with the men, and traveled with them until he came to the home of Cornelius, a Roman military captain, where a large crowd had gathered, and Peter was implored to come inside, eat, speak, and commune with them.

Peter said:

"You all know that it is against the Jewish laws for me to associate with or even visit the home of one who is not a Jew. Yet God has shown me that I should never view anyone as inferior or ritually unclean. [Nothing is unclean if God declares it to be clean.] So when you sent for me, I came without objection." (Acts 10:28).

Peter had to choose between the form of his devotion, and the deeper level of Chesed - loyalty, grace, and loving kindness. Some of us are so committed to the form, function, and structure of our faith, that we miss Spirit leading us beyond and through it all.

There's devotion to form, and there's living a life devoted to love and grace and kindness and growth. The main measure of your devotion to God is not your devotional life. It is simply your life. A devoted life is ever unfolding, always expanding, full of tension and wonder and discovery. Some might even call that a life of faith.

I wonder what Peter would have missed had he stuck to his convictions and denied the Roman military captain's invitation?

I wonder what we've missed as we've worried and stressed over how much of the Bible we've read, and how pure our prayers are?

DEVOTION - PART 5
An Honest Prayer

What does a devoted life look like?

Let's talk about prayer.

In her book, Help Thanks Wow, Anne Lamott said:

"My belief is that when you're telling the truth, you're close to God... So prayer is our sometimes real selves trying to communicate with the Real, with Truth, with the Light. It is us reaching out to be heard, hoping to be found by a light and warmth in the world, instead of darkness and cold... Light reveals us to ourselves, which is not always so great if you find yourself in a big disgusting mess, possibly of your own creation. But like sunflowers we turn toward light. Light warms, and in most cases it draws us to itself. And in this light, we can see beyond our modest receptors, to what is way beyond us, and deep inside." (2.)

Prayer connects us to what is beyond us and to what is deep inside us. That's why Paul encouraged his friends to "pray without ceasing." In other words, stay connected. In other words, stay honest. In other words, stay present.

Sometimes our 'form of devotion' is also a form of hiding. We hide in the success of making time for God, or shrink in our failure to do so. How do you 'make time' for the energy, essence, source, Divine God, who isn't just here, but is the here we find ourselves in?

You can't really make time for God, but you can choose to be awake, aware, and alive to God in you, around, and through you. And as Anne would say, sometimes our honest prayer is "help." I'm in the thick of it, and I don't know if God is real, or if love is true, but I'm here, and I could use a hand. Sometimes our honest prayer is "Thanks." Gratitude is a powerful force that brings us back to earth and changes our perspective. When we focus on the things we have, and not only on what we don't have, we see the world, others, and ourselves, more clearly. Sometimes our honest prayer is "wow." For when our words fail, and all we have is wonder, we are invited still to participate in the magnificence of it all with our bodies, eyes, thudding hearts, and pumping blood. That's a prayer, too.

And sure, there are moments where you "pray." where you say words and speak sentences that start with Dear God, and end with Amen. But as I continue to live into life, and become more honest, I find the poignant moments of prayer for me happen in between words, in the breath, in my decision to stay connected, honest, and present. After all, God is always paying attention to me. Not in a condescending, judgemental way… The prayer of God over my life is devotional. Chesed - loyalty, grace, loving kindness. Present to me, with me, and in me.

Sometimes, instead of making time to perform a devotional function of prayer, we would be better off staring our children in the face, eating a good meal, laughing with friends, telling the truth, and gazing at the stars, knowing that in them are the light of life, and in these honest experiences of grace and kindness, I am fully seen and fully known, and I can fully see and fully know right back.

"I DON'T KNOW EXACTLY WHAT A PRAYER IS. I DO KNOW HOW TO PAY ATTENTION, HOW TO FALL DOWN INTO THE GRASS, HOW TO KNEEL DOWN IN THE GRASS, HOW TO BE IDLE AND BLESSED, HOW TO STROLL THROUGH THE FIELDS, WHICH IS WHAT I HAVE BEEN DOING ALL DAY."
—Mary Oliver (3.)

> When you let go of what you think the Bible is, you are able to discover what it was always meant to be.

DEVOTION - PART 6

Humanity and Holiness

What does a devoted life look like?

Let's talk about the Bible.

The Bible is an ancient collection of stories, poems, histories, songs, biographies, visions, laws, precepts, genealogies, records, tales, and parables; a mixture of different genres and styles and form; written by many hands over many centuries, all brought together culminating into a crescendo of the greatest story ever explored:

What does it mean to be human? In a world with wars and violence and beauty and greed and pain and love and grace and mercy and justice or the lack thereof, and birth and death and illness and confusion and doubt and worry and joy and peace... in world full of everything we could imagine, and a lot of what we couldn't, what does it mean that there is a God of love who loves; who made us in love, by love, for love; and how does that relate to me and my life and the world around me?

The Bible is about the ongoing integration - or the continual awakening - of the holy and the human. We read about it starting with the creation poem Genesis; through the stories of Exodus, Abraham and Joseph; through the songs and liturgies in the Psalms; the truth of the prophets; the parables of Jesus; the memories of faithful friends and apostles.

It's not a list of rules or codes or commands that you can latch on to, learn, memorise, and stick to: follow the recipe and you'll get a perfect life and a grand old mansion in heaven.

Nope. When you let go of what you think the Bible is, you are able to discover what it was always meant to be. A book about how, from the very beginning, we've been trying to figure out who God is, and how we can live with each other well. It asks more questions than it gives answers. It actually provides room and expression for our doubts and confusion rather than shutting them down and voting them off the island. It includes our pain, draws it in close, and doesn't ask for it to be covered with a modesty cloth. This collection of books tackles humanities deepest questions about loss and anger and divinity and anxiety and violence and domination and money and stress and joy and grace and healing.

It's a story that continually affirms that the life we're trying to live as well and as honest and as true as we can is not futile, or a waste, or a hopeless collection of circumstances and atoms and bodies:

It is Divine.

In order to approach the Bible devotionally, look to the humanity and the holiness of it. Look to where it is pointing. And it's not pointing you in the direction of a quiet, lonely room, where you read 5 chapters, a commentary written by someone so far removed from its culture and context, a quick prayer, and then a check on the box on the list of 'how to be a good Christian.'

The Bible invites you into the kind of life its authors lived: the wrestle, the struggle, the joy, the misery, the challenge, the wonder of finding God in the middle, muck, and beauty of our own lives. And being found by grace in return. Or more honestly, realising that we have always been found.

If I could sum up Biblical devotion in a sentence, I would not do it anywhere near as much justice as Mary Oliver did when she wrote:

"Instructions for living a life.
Pay attention.
Be astonished.
Tell about it."

DEVOTION - PART 7
A Devoted Life

Is devotion a thirty-minute window of reading some verses, saying Dear God and Amen, and hoping you've done enough to stay in good graces for the day?

Devotion is the way of love. It's not something you do, it's something you become: A loving person.

What do you do when you're in love? When you say you're devoted to your children or your partner, what does that mean? What is it to be devoted to your sick parent, your best friend, your passion and vocation?

Devotion is about paying attention. When you love someone, you have more attention to give them. You are (ever on the journey of becoming more) aware of their needs, desires, dreams, fear, pain, and hopes.

To be devoted to God is to be loyal to life, devoted to love, yourself, and others, in all their fullness, in all the varying degrees and shade it all comes in, in the ways we can with what we have and what we know and the faith we choose to dive into. It's to pay attention, wake up, be aware and alive to The Divine-ness that is in us and beyond us. It's to savour this life; the moments, the gifts, the miracles, the longings, the hope... to give ourselves to each day and live it all the way through.

"The aim of God in history is the creation of an all-inclusive community of loving persons, with Himself included in that community as its prime sustainer and most glorious inhabitant." Said Dallas Willard. *"We must understand that God does not "love" us without liking us - through gritted teeth - as "Christian" love is sometimes thought to do. Rather, out of the eternal freshness of his perpetually self-renewed being, the heavenly Father cherishes the earth and each human being upon it. The fondness, the endearment, the unstintingly affectionate regard of God toward all his creatures is the natural outflow of what he is to the core - which we vainly try to capture with our tired but indispensable old word 'love'."*

Yes, devotion includes sacrifice and discipline and hard work. It includes silence and solitude and contemplation (If you've been reading me for a while, you'll know I'm all for that!). It includes correction and repentance and forgiveness.

Devotion includes the entirety of our lives - nothing is wasted, nothing gets left behind. But it does so in the pursuit of love, not perfection; to bring us close, not to shame us or make us feel unworthy; for the sake of healing, not exposing. A devoted life is led by love, in grace, through compassion and mercy.

Now, all this may sound slightly overwhelming: pay attention? All the time? Wide awake? What about Netflix?

That's part of paying attention: a devotional life includes time for rest and rejuvenation and even incubation where you heal and restore. If you're paying attention, you'll know what to do to be nurtured, and when to do it. And in turn, how to be there for others when they need the same.

And finally, your devotional life doesn't just include all the things you should/need/have to do for God. It's allowing yourself to be wrapped up and held in Divine love, too.

"God's love is meteoric,
his loyalty astronomic,
His purpose titanic,
his verdicts oceanic.
Yet in his largeness,
nothing gets lost;
Not a man, not a mouse,
slips through the cracks.
How exquisite your love, O God!
How eager we are to run under your wings,
To eat our fill at the banquet you spread
as you fill our tankards with Eden spring water.
You're a fountain of cascading light,
and you open our eyes to light."
Psalm 36:5-9 (MSG).

A devoted life is led by love, in grace, through compassion and mercy.

"WALK AS IF YOU ARE KISSING THE EARTH WITH YOUR FEET."

Thich Nhat Hanh

GET YOUR FIGHT BACK - PART 1
A Lover and a Fighter

How do you know when to fight and when to surrender?

How do you know how to fight and how to surrender?

I've spent much of my life fighting... fighting my way to the front of the crowd, fighting for jobs, for recognition, for my place in an institution... I've fought my brothers and family and friends and colleagues on matters of ethics and morality. I fought my science, history, and philosophy teachers (insert major facepalm here) on issues of creation and faith and trust. I've fought myself. For years I quietly, inwardly, struggled. I railed against my apparent sin-nature and inclination to do what was wrong. So much self-condemnation that I convinced myself was holy conviction. I fought the idea of who I was and who I was expected to be. I fought with my deepest self so that I could portray an image of a more acceptable and dynamic version of who I was.

So.much.fighting.

I got sick, physically and spiritually, and had to allow myself to go through the process of becoming well. I had to stop fighting and start surrendering to the reality of what was happening in and to me. I realised that one of the reasons I was so tired was that I was fighting the wrong battles and waging war on things that were meant to be loved. I've written about it before, and I'm writing about it again because, the season has once again changed, as they do, and I feel compelled to get my fight back.

Can the flow and the fight co-exist?

The Biblical text includes many stories and analogies and pictures around fighting. It's no wonder that being a 'Good Christian Soldier' is part of the language used in faith traditions the world over. But as with many things, our distance and ignorance of the culture and context these stories were written in has in many cases caused us to take things too far, like the idea that to be peacemakers we need to create culture wars and try to make others live like we do.

I'm on a mission to get my spark back, my grit and daring and boldness back. Maybe, like me, life has caused you to surrender, and you've had to lay so much down, you're not sure how to stand any more. Or perhaps, like me, you've grown tired of the constant bickering and competition and proving the 'Christian life' seems to be full of... you didn't sign up for that, and you're done with it. Or maybe, like how I feel in this season, you have this energy, a quickening of your spirit and pulse, an urgency to push through, not unlike the transition of labour when a woman gives birth; but you're not sure who you're fighting and what you're fighting for...

A passage of scripture that has been over and wrongly used so much that it's now a terrible cliché is helping me carve a way forward, it's guiding my energy, and I'd like to share with you how.

In Ephesians 6:10-20, Paul wrote to his friends and encouraged them to be strong and to pray and to put on the whole armour of God. It seems counterintuitive to armour up when healthy spirituality is about opening yourself to God and all that pertains to life. But there is a tension here to hold. We don't armour up to hide away our vulnerability, soft flesh, and the spots in our lives that are easily harmed. We armour up to STAY open, to stay in love, to keep generosity and empathy and kindness in our hands.

Because friends, what makes us strong isn't the ability to feel nothing, but the ability to feel everything and stay in the flow of love and grace. As Rumi said: *"Your greatest strength lies in the gentleness and tenderness of your heart."*

You can be a lover and a fighter at the same time.

GET YOUR FIGHT BACK - PART 2
Tell the Truth

How do you get your fight back?

Tell the truth.

A while back, on a weekend morning, I heard the terribly sad news that beloved author, mother, wife, friend, woman... Rachel Held Evans had passed away. I never knew Rachel, except through her blog and books and podcasts, but still, through her words, she had been a friend to me. A sister. I started to read the tributes — so many of them, and one of them, written by Sarah Bessey, said that above her writing desk hung a scribbled note that simply said: Tell the truth.

And that's what Rachel did. She told the truth, and it got her in trouble, it lost her money and friends and security and spots at certain conferences and shelf space at certain bookstores. But she did it anyway because truth builds integrity.

The Greek word for truth used in the New Testament is Aletheia, and subjectively it means "truth as a personal experience." Objectively, Aletheia is the truth and/or reality that is taught. In other words, it's something that we learn. In the ancient world, Rabbi's taught their disciples by taking them on the road so they would learn through the experience, through the living. It's the journey, the life we've lived; our truth. And yes, there is such a thing as your truth. You have your own personal truth about your experiences with God and life.

Truth is lived into. It's found in the ups and downs. It's not something you arrive at, it's something you continually discover.

Paul said:

"Put on God's complete set of armour provided for us, so that you will be protected as you fight against the evil strategies of the accuser! Your hand-to-hand combat is not with human beings, but with the highest principalities and authorities operating in rebellion under the heavenly realms... Put on truth as a belt to strengthen you to stand in triumph." (Eph 6:11-14 TPT.)

A belt builds core stability, integrity. It's not so much about wrapping an external truth around your life than it is about being truthful with your life. Tell the truth. Accept the truth. Be honest with yourself and with others. Be your own truth. Proudly. Softly. No Apologies. And stay open to learning more. This is how you build core strength, a belt if you will, into your life.

You know what's really triumphant? When you stop lying to yourself and others and God; when you can live your truth out in the open. That's how truth sets you free! Nothing to hide. Living in shadows, half concealed, is a prison no one should have to endure.

Please note: I'm not talking about flood-lighting... shocking people with the intimate details of your life and calling it truth telling. As Brené Brown said: *"Using vulnerability is not the same things as being vulnerable."* There are safe places and seasons and moments for all the different truths that are you.

You can't move forward until you make peace with the truth. And the truth is:

This is where you are.
You won't always be here.
Everything is temporary.
You can do hard things.
You were created for joy.
You are loved and valued.

Tell the truth. Live it, too. Wrap yourself up in it. This is how you get your fight back. Put away lies and propaganda and hiding and excuses. Don't keep your true self from the world because it might cost you money, fame, reputation... Don't put forward a construed version of yourself in the hopes of being more liked and accepted. Don't lie to stay out of trouble with the gate keepers and people on social media and certain members of your family. Make 'be kind and tell the truth' your personal mantra. Maybe scribble "tell the truth" on a note and hang it up where you'll see it every day. (Thank you, Rachel, for always telling the truth.)

GET YOUR FIGHT BACK - PART 3
Worthiness and Belonging

How do you get your fight back?

Stop hustling for your worthiness and accept the fact that you are holy and loved just as you are.

Paul said:

"Put on holiness as the protective armour that covers your heart." (Eph 6:14 TPT.)

How you hold your self reveals what you believe about yourself. Do you stand easy, owning your space? Or do you fold in on your chest?

In most faith traditions, we say things like: "Holy is the name of God, Holy are you, God." In the ancient world, your name was everything: your identity, your essence, and your reputation. It was more than a label - it carried our story with it. More than wealth and riches, the reputation of your name was the highest prize. When we say that God's name is Holy, we're making a statement about the identity, essence, and reputation of the Divine. God's name isn't a label, it carries the story of Divinity with it. It's alive with not just the idea of goodness, but the essence of it, too

Matt 6:10 says: *"Your kingdom come, your will be done, on earth as it is in heaven."*

God is holy, but God doesn't want to remain separate in God's holiness. "On earth as it is in heaven" is about the joining of the sacred and the human, the holy and the ordinary united. The incarnation is God declaring holiness within humanity.

"JUST TO BE IS A BLESSING. JUST TO LIVE IS HOLY."
— *Abraham Heschel.*

Humanity was always meant to embody the Divine, and the Divinely attributes of love and justice and generosity and thriving and compassion and peace. We don't become holy, we come to understand that we are. We don't work ourselves into a state of holiness, but when we realise that we are already holy, it changes the way we carry ourselves. It transforms us and the way we live.

In her book, An Altar in the World: A Geography of Faith, Barbara Brown Taylor said:

"No one longs for what he or she already has, and yet the accumulated insight of those wise about the spiritual life suggests that the reason so many of us cannot see the red X that marks the spot is because we are standing on it. The treasure we seek requires no lengthy expedition, no expensive equipment, no superior aptitude or special company. All we lack is the willingness to imagine that we already have everything we need. The only thing missing is our consent to be where we are."

We search beyond ourselves for meaning and worthiness and belonging. We want someone else to declare us holy, knight us, and send us on our way into the battle that life is. And all the while, our heart longs for us to stand easy, owning our own space, rather than folding in on our selves waiting for permission to believe we are who God says we are. What's missing is our consent to be where we are, to be who we are.

Stop hustling for your worthiness. Be willing to imagine that you already have everything you need. Straighten your chest that houses your holy heart. It's how you get your fight back.

"All we lack is the willingness to imagine that we already have everything we need. The only thing missing is our consent to be where we are."
— Barbara Brown Taylor

GET YOUR FIGHT BACK - PART 4

Enter into Peace

How do you get your fight back?

Generosity, empathy, connection... peace. They will get you back on your feet faster than anything else.

In part of his "armour" speech, Paul said:

"Wear on your feet the readiness that comes from the Good News of shalom [peace]." (Eph 6:15 CJB.)

We do all kinds of destructive things to "get ahead"- to come out in front, win the day, get back to a place of success, where we feel like we're 'winning.' But you don't have to scheme and steal and take, you don't have to push and strive and fake it... peace will get you back on your feet. Ironically, peace will get you your fight back.

Peace with yourself, and peace with others.

This peace is about connection. The Good News of The Gospel is less "here's your ticket to heaven," and more: "You belong here. You are loved. You are enough. God is with you, in you, for you. And there is plenty of God and belonging to go around... enough for all the world and back again."

That is the Good News of Peace - a declaration of the reality of oneness and connection that all living things and people share. And it changes everything.

Paul wants us to wear this good news on our feet so that we take it everywhere we go... into every situation, when we're alone and when we're with others. He wants us to wear it on our feet so that peace becomes foundational to our lives and our walk. Connection is everything. If we're not moving in the direction of deeper connection to ourselves, God, the earth, and others... what are we even here for?

Peace isn't something you achieve or acquire. It's something you enter into. You find it, discover it, uncover it. You cannot find peace by avoiding your life or conflict or disaster. But you can find peace within these things.

"YOU FIND PEACE NOT BY REARRANGING THE CIRCUMSTANCES OF YOUR LIFE, BUT BY REALIZING WHO YOU ARE AT THE DEEPEST LEVEL."
— *Eckhart Tolle.*

In her book Grounded: Finding God in the World-A Spiritual Revolution, Diana Butler Bass said:

"In the Bible, that vision is of a people who know God as an intimate companion, live well with one another, and fulfill God's dream for creation. It is a vision of mutuality, friendship, creativity, conviviality, and generosity. People are to make peace, plant vines and fig trees, treat one another fairly and with compassion, and invite strangers into God's tent. We are either cursed or blessed on the basis of our relationships with others and how we care for the land. People prosper when justice reigns. What is broken is restored, what is amiss is made right. It is a vision of a universal feast, a cosmic table around which all humankind is gathered to eat and drink and dance with God."

"WALK AS IF YOU ARE KISSING THE EARTH WITH YOUR FEET." — *Thich Nhat Hanh.*

(Wear on your feet the readiness that comes from the Good News of peace...)

That's how you get your fight back.

(And soon enough, the question becomes: what is the fight and what are we fighting for?)

GET YOUR FIGHT BACK - PART 5

Worthiness and Belonging

How do you get your fight back?

Have a little faith, dear one. Trust.

Paul wrote to his friends and said:

"With all these things, take up the shield of emunah (faith), by which you will be able to quench all the flaming darts of haRah (the Evil one)." (Eph 6:16 OJB.)

We don't give much room for mystery within the

mysteries and secrets that God is and does and declares throughout the world in a million different ways, most of which we miss because we're looking for something specific, labelled, explained, obvious... The Collective Church or Self Appointed Gate Keepers of Christianity encourage people to have faith, but then they also want to dictate what faith and trust look like: what your life will be like and look like if you have faith and if you trust God.

But we find God in the mystery. God dwells where we are least likely to look, transcending explanation and labels and logic and rules. If you can explain faith in seven dot points, it's not faith, it's religion. Faith isn't what you believe - that's dogma. Faith is HOW you believe.

In Hebrew, faith is the word "Emunah." In its original understanding, Emunah isn't about what you believe; it is beyond belief. It is an innate conviction, a perception of truth that transcends, rather than evades, reason.

Rabbi Tzvi Freeman said:

"Emunah is not based on reason. Reason can never attain the certainty of Emunah, since, reasonably speaking, a greater reasoning might always come along and prove your reasons wrong. In this way, Emunah is similar to seeing first hand: Reason can help you better understand what you see, but it will have a hard time convincing you that you never saw it. So too, Emunah endures even when reason can't catch up."

Emunah is the basis for the soul's relationship to spirituality. One who lives with Emunah is one who sees their existence firmly planted in The Divine. Emunah is not a destination, or a creed, or a label. It's what you journey with on your way to who knows where.

Too often, faith communities and groups become safe, predictable, controlled... reasonable: "You must have faith, and so that you know what that means, this is what it looks like and this is how you will behave, and this is how you will live". But faith can't be controlled. Faith has never been reasonable. It never will be.

How do you use faith like a shield? How do you pick it up and protect yourself with it?

Well, my friend, if I knew the answers, it wouldn't be faith at all.

What I can say is this: Trust the love you are held within. Spirit will lead you. Love will keep you. After all, love made Jesus do crazy things that seemed unfit for any reasonable saviour. If you journey with faith, it won't matter where you go. Faith always looks like a miracle. And who's to say how a miracle should behave?

The "the flaming darts of haRah (the Evil one)," are less little poisonous barbs shot at you from a little red man hiding in the shadows, aand more the whispers and temptations that say "you can't do it, you won't make it, and you're all alone." If the good news is that we all belong and that we all belong together, the "flaming darts of the evil one" are things that try and corrupt that belief, separate and divide us. Faith will always bring us together. Faith will always put your heart back together. Faith will always lead us to a greater sense of connection with others (regardless of what they believe), ourselves, the earth, and The Divine.

You can do this. You will get back up again. You belong here. You are enough. There is more for you. Believe that. Have faith. Trust in the love you are held within. This is how you get your fight back.

If the good news is that we all belong and that we all belong together, then the "flaming darts of the evil one" are things that try and corrupt that belief, to separate and divide us.

GET YOUR FIGHT BACK - PART 6
Rescued

How do you get your fight back?

Sometimes it takes a paradigm shift, a reworking of your why and what and where and when; "taking your thoughts and intentions and prejudices captive" if you will, to get your fight back. Sometimes it takes being saved from thinking that you have to fight for your place in the world.

Paul wrote to his friends and said: *"Embrace the power of salvation's full deliverance, like a helmet to protect your thoughts from lies."* (Eph 6:17 TPT.)

Salvations full deliverance? The concept of 'Salvation' deserves a series or five on it's on own. You might have noticed that I don't mention it a whole lot and that's simply because I don't believe salvation to be transactional; a ticket into heaven, a window seat on the glory train. I've heard preachers say that salvation is about being rescued from an eternity in hell; it's about being saved from your self; it's about being saved from the destruction of sin. To which I say: sure, fine, whatever.

I believe salvation to be much more holistic and down to earth. It's not a label that describes a singular experience. After all, Jesus came HERE, became one of US, and after he was brutally executed for treason by a foreign military superpower and his own colleagues, he rose again as a HUMAN. All good clues that salvation is a here and now thing, not a 'for later when we die' situation.

Barbara Brown Taylor said: *"Salvation is so much more than many of its proponents would have us believe. In the Bible, human beings experience God's salvation when peace ends war, when food follows famine, when health supplants sickness and freedom trumps oppression. Salvation is a word for the divine spaciousness that comes to human beings in all the tight places where their lives are at risk, regardless of how they got there or whether they know God's name. Sometimes it comes as an extended human hand and sometimes as a bolt from the blue, but either way it opens a door in what looked for all the world like a wall."* (1.)

When it comes to what is killing us, it almost always comes back to our perception and beliefs. Our beliefs around what is healthy and normal, who is deserving and who isn't (and that deserving is even a consideration), whether we are good or evil... we build for ourselves a prison within our hearts and minds, and our beliefs are, more often than not, the walls that keep us hemmed in and suffocating.

Embrace salvation's full deliverance, like a helmet to protect your thoughts from lies.

"SALVATION HAPPENS EVERY TIME SOMEONE WITH A KEY USES IT TO OPEN A DOOR HE COULD LOCK INSTEAD." — *Barbara Brown Taylor*. (Again! Isn't she brilliant?)

The lie that we are either in or out. The lie that we don't belong. The lie that there is only so much belonging to go around and we must wrestle it off others if we want in. The lie that fame and wealth make us worthy. The lie that we can't share this earth, our politics, and our towns with others who don't think or behave the same as we do. The lie that significance comes through what we do and not who we are. The lie that you are not enough.

Salvation doesn't save you from yourself, it rescues you to your true self: beloved, worthy of belonging, enough. It rescues you to others and the earth, too. And to The Divine. Salvation is the awareness that nothing can separate you from Divine love. Nothing. Salvation is the 'lived into' understanding that we all belong and that what we are fighting is not each other, but the limits we put on ourselves and others.

How do you get your fight back? Save yourself to yourself. Be rescued from thinking you have to fight others for your slice of the worthiness pie. Fight only your self imposed limits and prejudices that keep you from connecting.

"YOUR TASK IS NOT TO SEEK FOR LOVE, BUT MERELY TO SEEK AND FIND ALL THE BARRIERS WITHIN YOURSELF THAT YOU HAVE BUILT AGAINST IT."
— *Rumi.*

GET YOUR FIGHT BACK - PART 7

Aim Well and True

How do you get your fight back?

Choose a weapon. Aim true.

Paul wrote to his friends and said: *"And take the mighty razor-sharp Spirit-sword of the spoken Word of God."* (Eph 6:18 TPT.)

We've taken this verse to mean that 'The Bible' - the verses and words and lines - is our weapon. So in hard times, we've taken a verse and we've aimed it at whatever our perceived enemy has been. Popular enemies include: demons, people groups, other religions, governments, tyrants, people who don't live like us, and our own failed selves. Yep, we've even taken the words of the Bible and used them against ourselves, too... torn our hearts to pieces over how unworthy and unlovable we think it says we are.

But here's the thing: when Paul wrote this letter to his friends, there was no Bible. There was Torah, there were books of histories and prophets... there wasn't really a collected set of texts called The Bible that the Jewish people and the early Christians believed to be the "word of God." Paul may have been talking about something more than just some collected words on a page. After all, God and the Bible are not the same thing.

Richard Rohr said: *"The final and full Word of God is that spiritual authority lies not just in ancient texts but in the living Christ of history, church, community, creation, and our own experience confirming its truth. The mystery is "Christ among you, your hope of glory" (Colossians 1:27)—this is the living Bible! Keep one foot in both camps—the historical text and the present moment—and in your fullest moments you will find yourself also saying "it is like. . . ." Words are fingers pointing to the moon, but words are never the moon itself. Not knowing this has kept much religion infantile, arrogant, and even dangerous."* (3.)

When attempting to use the sword of the Spirit that is the word of God, ask yourself, what is the word of God? What does a word sound like out of the mouth of God, if God does indeed have a mouth and a voice?

I think it would sound like beauty and creativity and wonder. I think it would sound like healing and hope and redemption. I think it would sound like generosity and care and justice. I think it would sound like what the stories in the Bible are pointing to: a God who exists in all things and through all things who can be found anywhere by anyone at any moment. Words are fingers pointing to the Divine, but words are never the Divine itself.

"RAISE YOUR WORDS, NOT VOICE. IT IS RAIN THAT GROWS FLOWERS, NOT THUNDER." — *Rumi.*

Maybe the sword of the Spirit of the word of God is about actual words: words that bring life and love and grace and creativity... words that grow people and things and situations and yourself beyond where you are right now. But perhaps its more than words, too.

"EVERY CREATURE IS A WORD OF GOD." — *Meister Eckhart.*

Maybe the only weapon we really have is our life and the sound it makes, the creation that springs from its words, as we wield it around in the world. Eph 2:10 says: "We have become his poetry..." As with the Kingdom of God, the word weapon is not a sword that brings harm, but rather heals. Or I guess, that depends on how we use it.

How do you get your fight back? Don't just look to the book, look where the book is pointing: The Divine at home in the world, in our lives, in our very hearts. Raise your words, as in, raise the quality and the connectedness of them. Decide what you're fighting for, and who, and I hope you decide that you're fighting for yourself as much as anyone else, and that you're fighting the walls that would keep us disconnected; that the sound of your life would be a clarion call for belonging and healing and empowerment. And then, do your very best to aim well and true.

GET YOUR FIGHT BACK - PART 8
Willing to Cross

For a while there, the fight had gone from my life completely.

And to a point, it had to. I had spent so much of my life fighting. I fought myself sick and disillusioned, and sad, and lonely, and so very tired. I had to make friends with surrender and rest and stillness. Which I did. And that's a whole other story.

But now? I'm on a mission to get my spark back, my fight and grit and daring and boldness back. I've discovered that you can be a lover and a fighter at the same time. I've realised that you can rest and prepare at the same time. I'm learning that you can be both healing and hustling at the same time.

So, what exactly are we fighting for?

In Ephesians 6, Paul wrote to his friends and gave them an analogy to help explain what it's like to fight the fight of faith. He used items of armour as examples of things we need to put on and use in our lives. And in the end? All those pieces of armour and weaponry are a little contradictory in regards to their traditional use. On the spiritual path, they are used to keep us open, not guarded and closed. They are worn to protect us not from others, but from our propensity for greed and pride and isolation. They are used to bring us together, not drive us apart. In God's Kingdom, we don't fight each other, or others. We wrestle any barriers of love and grace that we have built against it inside of us. We fight the temptation to portray an image of who we think we should be. We fight the temptation to compare and compete and conquer. We fight the guilt and shame that would keep us isolated and projecting. We fight to be our true selves in a world that insists who we are isn't good enough.

Rumi said: *"Be like the sun for grace and mercy. Be like the night to cover others' faults. Be like running water for generosity. Be like death for rage and anger. Be like the Earth for modesty. Appear as you are. Be as you appear."*

When it comes to the devil, and the fiery darts of the evil one that Paul talks about in Ephesians 6, I think it's less about a little red man that has a horde of dark spirits doing his bidding which is always to tempt us to sin, and more about the opposition we face in allowing ourselves to be seen and known and loved, and the fear we have to see and know and love others. There isn't a single villain that can be our scapegoat for judgement and violence, there is only the wrestle to become human and holy in our own skin. The spiritual life is about taking responsibility for yourself, not abdicating it by having demons to blame for our troubles and a God to call upon to do the fixing for us.

Barbara Brown Taylor said: *"Once I gave up the hunt for villains, I had little recourse but to take responsibility for my choices... Needless to say, this is far less satisfying than nailing villains. It also turned out to be more healing in the end."* (4.)

This is how I fight my battles. I don't call on an invisible out there somewhere God to save me, do the work for me, take away my responsibility to myself and others. I allow Spirit to rise up in me, I connect to source - the flow of life that runs through my veins and fills my lungs and sparks my mind - and by harnessing that energy- by realising that I myself am a word of God - I empower my agency, intellect, empathy, courage... my hands and feet and eyes and ears and mouth.

And I fight my own battles. I do the work.

Because, dear friend, the armour is in you, and for you, and this battle can only be lived and fought and won, day in, day out, by you. The real you.

You can both pray and ask God for help, and fight your own battles at the same time.

That is how you get your fight back.

"RAISE YOUR WORDS, NOT YOUR VOICE. IT'S RAIN THAT GROWS FLOWERS, NOT THUNDER."

Rumi

NOTE TO SELF - PART 1
Raise Your Words

All-day every day, no matter where you are and what you're doing and who you're with and whether things are great or bad or average...

You are talking to yourself.

It's not only us crazies who do it... you do it, too. All of us, everyone. We all have an inner dialogue with ourselves about life and everything that happens in it. It's like a commentary, or a sports commentator calling the weekend game; an internal chatter about all the things we face: getting cut off on the freeway, having an argument with your partner, out to dinner with friends, not being able to find your socks... it seems that our inner self has something to say about everything whether we're conscious of it or not.

I became brutally aware of my inner voice about six years ago when I caught sight of my body in a mirror and felt like I was looking at a stranger. My inner voice went to work cutting that reflection, of a woman I felt I barely knew, down to size.

Things like:
Ugly
Incapable
Loner
Ignorant
Exhausted
Unlovable
Joke

I realised that as my inner voice told my body this information, my body accepted it as if it was gospel truth.

I had accepted other truths about myself over the years in different situations on both ends of esteem - often thinking I was nowhere near enough, and at times, that I was more enough than others. All these conversations I've had with myself, inside of myself.

I wonder what your inner voice sounds like?

In the last few lines of his letter to the Philippians, Paul told his friends to:

"Keep your thoughts continually fixed on all that is authentic and real, honorable and admirable, beautiful and respectful, pure and holy, merciful and kind..." (Phil 4:8 TPT.)

To which, if you're like me, we try to focus on authentic and real, honorable and admirable, beautiful and respectful, pure and holy, merciful and kind things outside of ourselves. Like God and angels and Mother Teresa and Keanu Reeves.

How often do you think 'authentic and real, honorable and admirable, beautiful and respectful, pure and holy, merciful and kind' things about yourself? From my experience, our inner dialogue tends to be more critical than not, when left to its own devices.

I grew up believing that to think of holy things is to think about God, not about self, because God is holy, and I am not. But it's not as black and white as that. God is within and without. God is the breath in my lungs and the blood in my veins and the energy that keeps this whole universe-world-thing going. And when I 'hear from God?' It is always within myself. How we treat, think about, and talk to ourselves, is a matter of holiness. Life flows from the heart, right? (Prov 4:23.)

How you speak to your 'self' matters. How you speak to your 'self' changes everything. Your internal dialogue can make or break you. Equally. And you don't have to be victim to whatever voice seems to be the dominant one inside your head.

I've learned (learning still) how to speak kindly and truthfully to myself. How to honour the sacredness of my body and personhood and treat her with respect and love and vulnerability. And it's healed me and woken me up and set me on a good path. You can learn it, too. Let me encourage you (and myself) down this path for the next little while.

"Raise your words, not your voice. It's rain that grows flowers, not thunder."
— Rumi.

Raise them to be words that are authentic and real, honorable and admirable, beautiful and respectful, pure and holy, merciful and kind... about you.

Start with you.

Start with the notes you send to yourself.

KINDNESS IS THE NATURAL
REACTION TO THE WORLD BY THOSE
WHO ARE FREE TO BE THEMSELVES.

NOTE TO SELF - PART 2
Beautifully Yourself

Note to Self: Your body is a wonderland.

Look, I couldn't help but write that line from one of John Mayer's first hits, but what I mean to say is:

YOUR.BODY.IS.GOOD.

Not only is your body good, your body is a someone. It is not an 'it,' a thing, a tool, an object. Your body is wonderful and holy and incredible. It's soft and strong, resilient and fragile, wise yet still learning, all at the same time. Your body was created, and designed, to feel pleasure and enjoy it. To keep you safe from harm, to nurture and love others, to work and rest and play and revel and eat and protest and dance and run and stretch and give and receive... Your body is what feels the warm afternoon sun prickle down your arms, and it is your body that feels the cool evening breeze that shivers up your back. It is your body that dives deep into the ocean. It is your body that sits at a desk learning, it is your body that is held by your lover's body, and it is your body that holds others. It is your body that carries you across rooms and oceans to reach out and contribute and help. And it is your body that others arrive to, to nurture and strengthen.

Your body is not inherently evil.
Your body is not unholy.
Your body isn't just a tool for while you're here on earth.
Your body is not collateral damage for the sake of some kind of calling.
Your body is not irrelevant.
Your body is you and you are beautiful and you are holy.

Your body tells the truth of who you are and what is going on inside you, and even around you. If you're not tuned in, not only will you miss out on vital information your self is trying to tell you, but you'll miss one of the most loving relationships you were created to have: with your own body and self.

And when I say your body, I mean, your body as it is right here, right now. That body, this body, your body, is worthy of love; is loveable. Whether you are in good or ill health, whether you think you're beautiful according to the ridiculous and narrow narratives of whoever from where ever. Whether you have been mercilessly used up by others, or whether you've been loved your whole life long. No matter what your inner dialogue has been about the flesh and blood that house your heart and soul, you can make a commitment to your precious flesh at this moment, wherever you are reading this devotion, to love him or her the way she or he is loved by the Divine, God-self.

"We cannot return to a healthy view of our own bodies until we accept that God has forever made human flesh the privileged place of the divine encounter..." Said Richard Rohr (1). *"We have had enough of dualism, enough of the separation of body and spirit, enough over-emphasis on the body's excesses and addictions. We must reclaim the incarnation as the beginning point of the Christian experience of God. The embodied self is the only self we have ever known. Our bodies are God's dwelling place and even God's temple (see 1 Corinthians 6:19-20)."*

Your body is good. Your body is where you find God, is how you find God. Where else do you experience the fullness of Presence (a divine encounter) other than with and in your own body?

To be beautiful means to be yourself. You don't need to be accepted by others. You only need to be accepted by yourself.

What notes will you write to your body? What words will you use?

Because, of course, you can choose.

NOTE TO SELF - PART 3
Thank God You've Changed

Note to self: You don't have to be who you've always been.

"You've changed.
You're not the same as you used to be.
I thought you'd be different."

Thank God for that.

Because if someone has said that to you, it's most likely not because you're flakey, or you've done something wrong, or you're in-authentic. It's that you've followed the natural progression of things. You've grown. You've learned. You've moved forward. You've progressed, evolved, changed. You are continually becoming.

Just because you used to believe one thing, had a particular role or job, fulfilled something for others, doesn't mean you have to keep on doing that.

You are allowed to change.
You are allowed to change your mind.
You are allowed to change your beliefs.

You are allowed to live into your questions and answers even if they take you down unexpected roads and pathways. Especially if they take you down unexpected ways.

"I WANT TO UNFOLD.
I DON'T WANT TO STAY FOLDED ANYWHERE,
BECAUSE WHERE I AM FOLDED, THERE I AM A LIE."
— *Rainer Marie Wilke.*

Stagnation is a silent killer. It will stiffen your heart and stifle your dreams. It will slow your productivity and taint your contribution. You were made to move and flow like a river that is constantly pouring itself out onto new shores.

"We do not grow absolutely, chronologically." Said Anais Nin. "We grow sometimes in one dimension, and not in another; unevenly. We grow partially. We are relative. We are mature in one realm, childish in another. The past, present, and future mingle and pull us backward, forward, or fix us in the present. We are made up of layers, cells, constellations."

So dear friend, don't feel trapped into a personality or a vocation or a belief system just because you've chosen it before and you think consistency is what gives you authority and value.

It's your consistent surrender to the movement of life that will see you continually become who you're meant to be, flowing down that river of change and grace.

Anais Nin went on to say:

"And the day came when the risk to remain tight in a bud was more painful than the risk it took to blossom."

Thank God you've changed. Thank God you continue to change. You don't have to be who you've always been. Be free to be who you are in this moment, and then to shed your skin and keep on growing when the moment moves on.

NOTE TO SELF - PART 4
You're a Living Revelation

Note to self: God is not angry with you.

Your life isn't an exercise in making up for your sins and fallenness. You don't have to prove yourself worthy, or faithful, or pure to appease God and receive Divine love. Jesus' blood is not on your hands.

Let me say it again: God is not angry with you.

I grew up believing that my whole life was an offence to God. That's what they taught at my church, and that's the story I was told at home. Me, my body and mind and thoughts and words: offensive. Unless I was "washed by the blood of the lamb," which I inadvertently killed because of my sin. If it weren't for me, Jesus wouldn't have had to die. So I should be thankful. And I should do better. And I should live a life worthy of the call. And I should repent when I don't, but also when I'm not sure, just in case.

What a toxic cycle of pleasing and striving and working for something I had all along:

The love and grace of God the Divine energy that got this whole thing started, and keeps this whole thing going, including me.

God is not angry with you.

"The common Christian reading of the Bible is that Jesus "died for our sins" —either to pay a debt to the devil (common in the first millennium) or to pay a debt to God the Father (proposed by Anselm of Canterbury, 1033-1109)." Wrote Richard Rohr in his book, Things Hidden. *"Theologians later developed a "substitutionary atonement theory"—the strange idea that before God could love us, God needed and demanded Jesus to be a blood sacrifice to "atone" for our sin. As a result, our theology became more transactional than transformational.*

Franciscan philosopher and theologian John Duns Scotus (1266-1308) was not guided by the Temple language of debt, atonement, or blood sacrifice (understandably used in the New Testament written by observant Jews). He was instead inspired by the cosmic hymns in the first chapters of Colossians and Ephesians and the first chapter of John's Gospel. For Duns Scotus, the incarnation of God and the redemption of the world could never be a mere mop-up exercise in response to human sinfulness, but the proactive work of God from the very beginning. We were "chosen in Christ before the world was made" (Ephesians 1:4). Our sin could not possibly be the motive for the divine incarnation; rather, God's motivation was infinite divine love and full self-revelation! For Duns Scotus, God never merely reacts, but always freely acts out of free and unmerited love.

Jesus did not come to change the mind of God about humanity (it did not need changing)! Jesus came to change the mind of humanity about God. God's abundance and compassion make any scarcity economy of merit or atonement unhelpful and unnecessary. Jesus undid "once and for all" (Hebrews 7:27; 9:12; 10:10) all notions of human and animal sacrifice and replaced them with his new infinite economy of grace."

Of course, you will find scripture that seems to refute that. But suffice to say for now that scripture is a becoming, an unfolding story of God revealed to humanity IN humanity, and how humanity interpreted that through the changing contexts of culture and time. The language does its best, but it is not the pinnacle of revelation, it can only point in the right direction, which it does through the whole story, not just the words.

Here's a good place to start:

"But Lord, your nurturing love is tender and gentle. You are slow to get angry yet so swift to show your faithful love.

You are full of abounding grace and truth."
Ps 86:15 (MSG).

You don't have anything to make up for. You do not have to try and appease an angry God with righteous living. That kind of life will twist you up inside and suck the life right out of you.

Your life is a manifestation, a living revelation, a witness and a testimony of the love you were made of and in and with and for.

NOTE TO SELF - PART 5
Nothing to Prove

Note to self:

Rest and be kind. You don't have to prove anything. (via Jack Kerouac).

You don't have to prove anything.
You don't have to prove anything.
You don't have to prove anything.
You don't have to prove anything.
You don't have to prove anything.

Life is a gift, and it's yours for the taking, not the earning. You are already beloved of God. You are already held by grace. You already belong, as you are with all you are.

You are free from having to earn or prove your place in the world.

Which makes you free to rest and free to be kind.

Rest, friend. Rest. Jump off the treadmill of approval. Resist the urge to puff yourself up and prove yourself worthy by your successes and accumulations and titles. All that stuff can get destroyed in a second. You need something more substantial to hold you up, like your own heart and soul and body.

Rest. Rest because you need it. Rest because your contribution to the world needs you strong and big-hearted and empowered by a full night's sleep. Rest because you're not loved any more by working yourself to the bone.

Be kind.

When you can rest in the awareness that you have nothing to prove and nothing to earn, kindness is no longer threatening or exhausting or a gamble. Kindness is the natural reaction to the world by those who are free to be themselves.

Unthreatened by the position or assumptions or opinions of others, those who have nothing to prove are free to be generous.

So you, your self, my self:

Rest and be kind. You have nothing to prove.

"Rest and be kind, you don't have to prove anything."
— Jack Kerouac

NOTE TO SELF - PART 6

You've Got This

Note to self: You've got this.

Because who else is going to do it? Who else can traverse the wild landscape of your life other than you?

Who else can go through your highs and lows, successes and failures, other than you?

You've got this.

Of course, you do. You can do hard things. Yes, there is a beautiful fragility to your heart and life, but you also have grit and courage and strength. Beneath the soft tissue of your chest and stomach and pelvis is your spine. Your backbone. It holds you together. Let it awaken to its true purpose of strength and vitality.

You've got this.

Look, I know some people say: God's got this. And that's true. God, Divine energy, the source that got this world started, the groundedness that keeps it together, and the creativity that keeps it all moving forward - God's got this. God's got you. In the sense that the same power that raised Christ from the dead is in you (Romans 8:11). As in, it's a part of you. As in, you are in control of how you steward your life. 'The power' doesn't do it for you. The power is in you waiting for you to take full responsibility for your own life. Then, and only then, can it get to work on your behalf.

I grew up a Pastor's kid, and was a Pastor myself for a long while. I've been to all the conferences and concerts and events... I couldn't tell you how many prayer meetings and worship services I've been involved in and subjected myself to. I've met the famous and the sanctified, and I've been blessed and anointed.

And yet things didn't change for me, they didn't start working for me, until I started to take 100% responsibility for my own life. I stopped waiting for God to do everything for me and began to trust that the Divine works through me and with me instead.

This doesn't mean becoming an island. Responsibility doesn't isolate you, it's quite the opposite. Because I took responsibility for my life, I was more intentional about surrounding myself with gracious and loving people. Because I took responsibility for my life, I realised that I can't do it by myself, so I reached out for help and wisdom and companionship in a healthy way, rather than in some interdependent passive-aggressive formula.

You are the steward of your own life.

And you've got this.

"*Yes, people disappoint you.*" Said Liz Gilbert... "*Yes, people can hurt you horribly. Yes, the world is unfair and sometimes cruel — but that has always been part of the contract. (It's not even in the small print: It's pretty much the bold print headline of the contract.) The world never pretended or promised anyone that it would not sometimes be terribly unfair and cruel [neither did Jesus] or at least that it would not sometimes be utterly incomprehensible.*"

And yet still,

You are the steward of your own life, your reactions and responses.

And you've got this.

Going through divorce?
You've got this.
In pain?
You've got this.
Confused? Need answers?
You've got this.
Feeling detached and mediocre?
You've got this.
Lonely? Need a friend?
You've got this.
In the middle of a horrible disagreement?
You've got this.
Feel disempowered?
Not sure what you believe?
Politically and spiritually?
Broken and hurt?
Determined and enduring?
Goal in sight?
Dream stirring in the heart?

YOU.HAVE.GOT.THIS.

And you're not alone.

The same power that rose Christ from the dead is in you - as in, its a part of you, it lives in your backbone and heart and spirit, you breathe it in and out of your lungs, and it pumps through your body in platelets and cells, so much so that you can't tell where it ends and you begin - to empower YOU to have agency over your own life.

These days, when I ask myself in those hard and messy situations: Who's got this?

Somewhere deep inside, the best and wisest part of me rises up and says,

I do.

You've got this friend, whatever this is.

And we've got your back.

NOTE TO SELF - PART 7
Doing Their Best

If how you talk to yourself, about yourself, has the power to change your life, then what about the things you say to yourself about others?

What notes to yourself are you writing about your neighbour? Your kid's friends? Your partner? Your colleagues? People on the internet?

And look, I get it. It's completely naive to think that we should only have nice, fluffy things to say about everyone. Because honestly, some people do nasty and horrible things and words need to be said it (and actioned, too).

If you think of your inner dialogue as creating a foundation of attitude and direction for your life, then it's just as important that your inner dialogue is as true as it is compassionate. Somehow we need to hold the tension of truth-telling and grace, justice and compassion, grief and healing… maybe they don't all come at the same time. I know anger needs to be expressed because some things should make you angry. I know that confrontations need to happen because some times you need to stand up for yourself, or for others. Protesting is holy. Raising your voice is holy. Telling the truth is holy.

So how do we create a foundation in our heart for ourselves and others that leans towards growth and healing and wholeness? Even in the midst of the horrific and heartbreaking things that others say and do?

There's no easy answer. And there is no dot point list or spiritual key or magic prayer that will make it all clear and black and white.

But recently, on Russell Brand's podcast 'Under the Skin', Brené Brown spoke about this very thing. She said that she could find God and love in anybody. Even offensive people, even people who we might think are doing horrific things. In a study she conducted, she asked people to think of the very worst person they could and ask themselves if they thought that person was doing the very best they could. And then she asked them to imagine God telling them that that person WAS doing the very best they could.

It's a hard question. Because if you answer yes, you believe that people are doing their best, what does that mean in regards to your pain and suffering? In regards to the injustice and tragedies perpetrated throughout the world? And for the things you and I are trying to change?

Brené said she asked her husband, Steve, what he thought, "Are people doing the best they can?" He took his time and came back to her and said: "I have no idea, but what I do know is that my life is better when I believe that they are." (2.)

Maybe we should believe that they are, as hard as that may be, if only for this: it generates compassion and empathy and reason in our hearts. It leads us somewhere creative and life-generating.

Bitterness will twist you up. Judgement is a two-edged sword.

But you can tell the truth to yourself about someone, and give yourself the grace to not have to understand it or fix it or make it right. You can choose to believe that in that person's belief system, value framework, set of experiences and circumstances, they probably are doing the best they can, even if we can't see it for all the love and light in the world.

And for some reason, that helps.

As Heschel said, "words create worlds." (3.) The notes you leave your body, soul, and heart, about yourself and others, are building yours. What will you say?

Note to self: People are doing the best they can.

FAITH IS A KIND OF KNOWING THAT DOESN'T NEED TO HOLD EVERYTHING ITSELF BECAUSE, AT A DEEPER LEVEL, IT KNOWS IT IS BEING HELD.

Richard Rohr

ROOM FOR MYSTERY - PART 1

When You Open Your Heart

It's in our nature to want to solve a mystery. There's a reason Agatha Christie was such a successful novelist (apart from the fact that she was a brilliant writer). We turn page after page after page in anticipation of solving the mystery. Who did it? When? With what? Mystery solved.

Many of us live as if we've solved the mystery of God. We love to talk about the Divine in definitive terms. God does this, and not that, God is this, and not that: explain God, box God, package God up and turn God into a neat and tidy "product."

But God is more like an Indie film than an Agatha Christie Novel: endlessly mysterious, perhaps even strange. Ultimately unknowable. If we treat God like a mystery that is solved, a lesson we've already learned, a book we've read and have committed to memory, then we know less about the Divine then we think we do.

Much less.

Richard Rohr said:

"We all need, forever, what Jesus described as 'the beginner's mind' of a curious child. A beginner's mind is the best path for spiritual wisdom. Tobin Hart writes: "Instead of grasping for certainty, wisdom rides the question, lives the question. When the quest for certainty and control is pushed to the background, the possibility of wonder returns. Wonder provides a gateway to wise insight." Incorporating negative and self-critical thinking is essential to true prophetic understanding. At the same time, we must also trust that we are held irrevocably in the mystery of God's love, without fully understanding it.

Alongside all our knowing, accompanying every bit of our knowing, must be the humble 'knowing that we do not know.' That's why the great tradition of prayer is balanced by both kataphatic knowing, through images and words, and apophatic knowing, through silence, images, and beyond words.

Apophatic knowing is the empty space around the words, allowing God to fill in all the gaps in an 'unspeakable' way.

Strangely enough, this unknowing is a new kind of understanding. We have a word for it: faith, a kind of knowing that doesn't need to know and yet doesn't dismiss knowledge either; a kind of knowing that doesn't need to hold everything itself because, at a deeper level, it knows it is being held." (1.)

Wisdom isn't something that happens when you know it all. Wisdom is what happens when you open your heart up to curiosity and wonder. Wisdom lives the questions... it doesn't profess it knows the answer to everything.

"Wonder rather than doubt is the root of all knowledge."
— *Rabbi Abraham Joshua Heschel.*

It's the tension between knowing and not knowing. Living into the questions, rather than needing a prescriptive answer. Getting immersed in the mystery knowing that you may not ever come to the absolute end of it.

In Exodus chapter three, Moses asked God,

"When I'm asked who you are, what should I say?"
God replied with this phrase:
"Ehyeh aŝer ehyeh."
Which most closely means:
"I am who I am."
(and/or)
"I will be what I will be."

How do you box that into a definition?

Some theological practices say that we make an idol out of our concepts of who God is. Trying to explain and define the Divine exclusively and concretely is itself idolatry.

God is not a mystery to be solved, but one to enjoy and explore.

ROOM FOR MYSTERY - PART 2
Keep on Looking

I used to think I knew all the answers. As a Pastor, and a long time spiritual know-it-all (I'm in recovery now), people would come to me with questions, and I would fire off answers. About God, sin, forgiveness, life... all of it.

But I was missing something: wonder.

Of course, we all believe the words of Isaiah 55:8-9:

"For my thoughts are not your thoughts, neither are your ways my ways," declares the Lord. "As the heavens are higher than the earth, so are my ways higher than your ways and my thoughts than your thoughts."

But instead of allowing this verse to make room for wonder, we use it to shut down curiosity:

"Don't bother asking, cos we'll never understand.

God's ways are higher than ours."

We've used it as a prescription to cover up questions and the beautiful space of unknowing.

Why did God want the Israelites to kill all the women and children, too? God's ways are higher...
Why did my Dad get cancer? God's ways are higher...
Why did Jesus heal some people are not others? God's ways are higher...
Why do we accept these people, and not those people? God's ways are higher.

Ironically, we've used this beautiful verse about wonder to shut conversations down, rather than open them up.

What if you didn't HAVE to have an answer for anything? What if you could ask your questions without getting shut down? What if you started to live your way into the answers?

Enter, silence.

A few years back, prayer started to change for me. I began to sit in silence more than in hurried and urgent chatter. It was meditative. And restful. Mysterious. Beautiful. I took the time to actually "be still and know that God is God."(Ps 46:10.)

But in the "knowing that The Divine is God" bit, came a tremendous realisation of how much I didn't know. It was as if I was asking God, "who are you?" And he was replying with:

"I am who I am, and I will be what I will be." (Exodus 3:14.)

A little further on from the story of Moses and the Burning Bush in Exodus 3, Moses was in the desert with the Israelites. God kept on talking to him about taking the people to the promised land, and in Exodus 33, Moses had this discourse with God:

"Show me your glorious presence."

It's as if he'd been asking: Who are you, and how will I know, how can I be sure?

And The Divine answered with this:

"Look, stand near me on this rock. As my glorious presence passes by, I will hide you in the crevice of the rock and cover you with my hand until I have passed by. Then I will remove my hand and let you see me from behind. But my face will not be seen."

If I were Moses, I would be mad. How many times have we prayed: How can I be sure? Show me what to do? Give me the answer?

And have been met with silence?

There's an old Jewish Midrash, a commentary written by wise Rabbi's, where they said that what God more or less told Moses: The best kind of certainty you'll get is that you'll be able to see where I just was..."

HOW INFURIATING. At least it is for those of us who want concrete, hard evidence, right here, right now.

But think about it. How else do you glimpse the Divine mystery than by seeing its imprint on your life, the lives around you, the world around, as if it had just been there one second before you arrived?

The challenge is to keep on looking. Don't let the absence of answers defeat you. Let them enliven you. Stoke up the fires of curiosity and wonder and follow that mystery with everything you have.

"God's ways are higher" isn't the end of the conversation. It's the beginning.

ROOM FOR MYSTERY - PART 3
The Freedom to Ask

There's a story in Mark's memoir where Jesus crossed over to the other side of the lake, and a storm rose up and near shook the life out of them.

The disciples raged Jesus awake and begged him to save them. Which he did. He spoke to the storm, and the wind and the waves submitted themselves to peace and calm. After everything had settled, Jesus turned to his friends and said:

"Why are you so afraid? Haven't you learned to trust yet?" (Mark 4:40 TPT.)

Other translations say, *"Do you still have no faith?"* (NLT.)

That response fits so well with God's answer to Moses when he asked,

"Who shall I say sent me?"
(God replied:)
"I am who I am."

Haven't you learned to trust, yet?

There's a certain amount of "letting go" involved in faith. I know Hebrews 11:1 says that "faith is the evidence of things unseen," but can't you see the irony in that? I think the writer of Hebrews may have been laughing to himself when they wrote it...

The evidence of faith is the willingness to sit with ambiguity, to pursue truth rather than attain it, and to hold the tension of knowing and 'unknowing' in both hands. To do this, you have to let go of not only the idea but also the stance of being "right," and embrace your humanity and humility.

In Matthew 18:3, Jesus said: *"Learn this well: Unless you dramatically change your way of thinking and become teachable, and learn about heaven's kingdom realm with the wide-eyed wonder of a child* (HELLO, CURIOSITY), *you will never be able to enter in. Whoever continually humbles himself to become like this gentle child is the greatest one in heaven's kingdom realm."*

Kids are insatiably curious. They ask endless questions, explore the nitty-gritty, and instead of getting embarrassed or regretful at what they find or hear or learn, they usually just laugh and laugh and laugh.

And then ask more questions...

The best parenting advice I received when I was pregnant with my first child was this: Let your child know how much you love them. Don't worry so much about boundaries, and do's and don'ts and if they'll go too far, or not far enough. Children who feel secure in love have a curious freedom that serves them well.

Curiosity is fortified by trust. A holy curiosity, a divine vocation of learning, is empowered by faith. A faith that says, "there is more going on here than I currently know." And perhaps, more than I can ever know.

Divine love doesn't answer all your questions, it gives you the freedom to ask every single one of them.

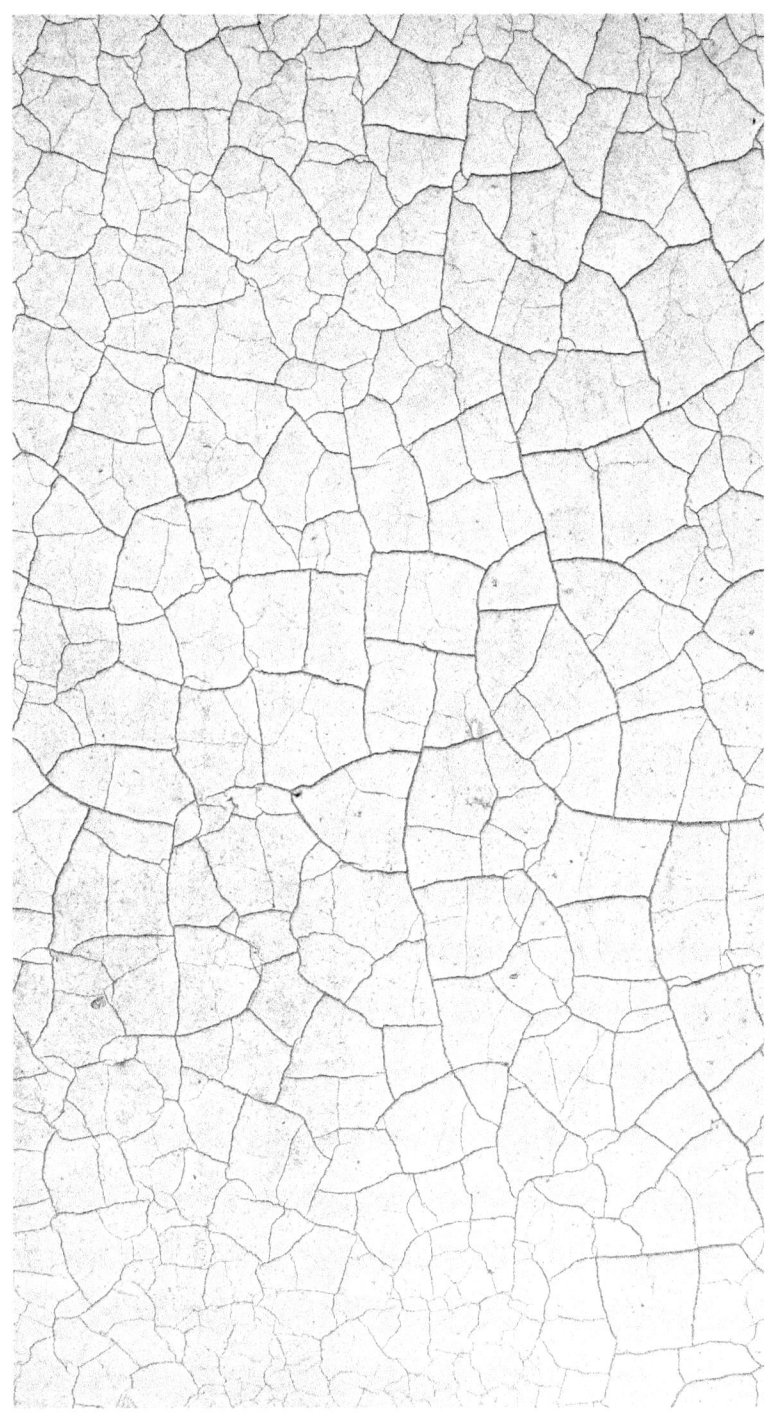

Divine love doesn't answer all your questions, it gives you the freedom to ask every single one of them.

ROOM FOR MYSTERY - PART 4
Engaging Wonder

Silence is a form of prayer.

If prayer is just about sending God our list of the things we want, and people we want smote, and what we want God to do for us and to others, then we are missing the point entirely.

Prayer is flow, relationship, awareness, laughing, crying, speaking a little, listening a lot... to pray is to give yourself over to the belief that you are sharing this moment with the essence of all things. Source. And that the source of all things is sharing back with you. A beautiful and holy exchange.

In this place of surrender, what we know and what we do not know can live at ease with each other – there is no competition.

Prayer is the gateway to wonder.

Richard Rohr said (quote from Part One):

"At the same time, we must also trust that we are held irrevocably in the mystery of God's love, without fully understanding it. Alongside all our knowing, accompanying every bit of our knowing must be the humble 'knowing that we do not know.' That's why the great tradition of prayer is balanced by both kataphatic knowing, through images and words, and apophatic knowing, through silence, images, and beyond words. Apophatic knowing is the empty space around the words, allowing God to fill in all the gaps in an 'unspeakable' way." (2.)

I think we have the "kataphatic knowing" down pretty well. We are quick to rattle off what we KNOW about God and what God does and doesn't do, say, believe, and behave.

But to sit with the unknown? To engage mystery and wonder? Even the idea that what we think we know about God might be incomplete?

That's a humility that our culture, and our generation, finds uncomfortable.

Apophatic Prayer emphasizes loving silence and "unknowing." It's surrendering our language, awareness, and understanding over to God's infinite nature. It knows God through absence and silence, mystery and darkness. Not in an evil sense, but in an "unknown" sense... think 'Interstellar.'

There is an eternal 'more' to what we already think we know. We get stuck on definitions and party lines and right and wrong and knowledge and light and clarity, that we've almost crowded out any space for wonder. For the absence of answers, and our acceptance of that absence.

Because ultimately, we don't trust that the more beyond what we know is good, and worth pursuing, and attainable. We don't trust beyond what we know. Which is kinda the opposite of faith...

Prayer is the place where this comes to fruition for me. Whether it's more meditative and silent, or a hurried plea for help: I bring what I know about God, and life and love, and I allow space for what I don't know to breathe and move in and around my situation.

"Allowing God to fill in all the gaps in an 'unspeakable' way."

ROOM FOR MYSTERY - PART 5
A Way of Being

When we let go of our need to be right and certain and to know everything, we simultaneously make room for the unexpected. For the possibility of something beyond what we know and have experienced. Something beautiful happens when we surrender our "rightness" and let go of the need to know everything.

It helps us see other people as, simply, other people. Not enemies or adversaries, but people made of flesh and blood and bone and breath, just like us.

Rigid and staunch faith has no movement or flexibility… no life. It's flat and arid.

But a faith that includes un-knowing? That acknowledges our finite nature alongside infinite divinity? A faith that trusts there is more going on here than what we know?

Look, real faith is a risk. It requires a level of brokenness, humility, and courage. All expansion does.

In 2 Corinthians, Paul said that God said to him:

"My grace is always more than enough for you, and my power finds its full expression through your weakness." So I will celebrate my weaknesses, for when I'm weak I sense more deeply the mighty power of Christ living in me. So I'm not defeated by my weakness, but delighted!"

Rumi said kind of the same thing:

"THE WOUND IS THE PLACE THE LIGHT ENTERS YOU."

Some of us use certainty to cover our wounds. Pride is a crude bandage for our suffering, and yet, we cling to it. But grace is more than enough…

Grace isn't some quick fix script that the Divine bestows upon us so that we may approach. Grace is something we live into, and with. It's a way of being, of letting go, of trusting. "I'm wounded, yet somehow, someway, I'm still strong." Grace is the light entering you through your wounds.

Grace is letting go of the need to be wound-less.

The acknowledgment of our weakness, of our wounded-ness, make us stronger. "Here is what I know, and here is what I don't know." (Not that you can articulate what you don't know, because then you would know it, but you know what I mean…) It's in the admission of our finiteness that we can explore the infinite.

Humility isn't a passive emotion. It's a robust and vital way of living open-handed and hearted. It says "I don't know what's going on here, but I want in on it anyway."

It's in the letting go of our need to be right and certain and whole and to know everything, that we simultaneously make room for the unexpected, that we begin to live some kind of way into the answers.

A lifetime of it.

ROOM FOR MYSTERY - PART 6
Held in the Mystery

"For now we see but a faint reflection of riddles and mysteries as though reflected in a mirror, but one day we will see face-to-face. My understanding is incomplete now, but one day I will understand everything, just as everything about me has been fully understood. Until then, there are three things that remain: faith, hope, and love—yet love surpasses them all. So above all else, let love be the beautiful prize for which you run." 1 Cor 13:12-13 (TPT).

Faith knows that we CAN see. We've experienced the divine in varying degrees and in different ways all on our own. But for all our study and experience and understanding, it's still just a "faint reflection" - riddles and mysteries as though reflected in a mirror... [it is yet] incomplete.

We can't prove it or even properly articulate it. With all its words and rules and ways, language still fails us when it comes to putting verbal substance to divinity.

Trust takes hold of the "until then" bit of the scripture in 1 Corinthians. It pursues faith, hope, and love. It holds our need to know, and a "non-need" to know in a divine tension, keeping us humble and seeking.

I've mentioned Apophatic Prayer a few times through this series. It explores the Divine by focusing on what/who God isn't, and allows room for what is beyond our understanding. It's often silent, meditative.

God is the ground of your own being – the glue – the presence at the heart of all things, a saturating and engulfing love. No words can express this, and so Apophatic Prayer emphasizes loving silence and "unknowing" as distinctive features. It makes room for mystery in the absence of definition.

There's an apophatic prayer that a group called "The Liturgists" released on an album a couple of years ago, that I found restorative in my faith journey.

It starts with a statement about who God is:
"God is our father."

For some, this is comforting and reassuring. But for others, depending on their personal experiences with their father, this could be a difficult phrase to say. As you pray it, different images and pictures will come to mind of what it looks like for God to be your father.

The next phrase is a negation of the first:
"God is not our father."

Before you freak out, it's true. God is NOT our father. The Divine isn't a male human who fathered us with someone else. God doesn't tell Dad jokes and work the BBQ. God isn't a father. God is more than a father. The language of "father" is too limiting for who God is in God's entirety.

Therefore, the next line is:
"God is not our father, for God is more than our father."

The next phrase sounds uncomfortable at first, but it's my favorite. It hints at possibility and wonder and hope.
"God is not, not our father."

Yep, no typo: two "nots." In the apophatic tradition, this is where the power lies. The idea of God NOT being a father, or being more than a father is still confined to our human understanding and language.

"By saying "God is not, not our Father", we come to the end of language. We admit that our thoughts can't define God, and further that they can't even describe their own limitations. To the mystics, we perhaps are now present with God. Here in the lack of any understanding. Here in the murkiness of mystery, when we have stopped making an idol of God with our concepts and language... we are finally just present with the great "I will be who I will be."" – Mike McHargue.

We are held irrevocably in the mystery of God's love, without fully understanding it.

God is Ehyeh asher ehyeh:

"I am who I am, and I will be what I will be." (Ex 3:14.)

Make room for the mystery.

Sit with this prayer, and add in your own phrases following the same pattern. Or you can find this prayer on Spotify like I did. Just look up "The Liturgists."

> "Here in the lack of any understanding. Here in the murkiness of mystery, when we have stopped making an idol of God with our concepts and language… we are finally just present with the great "I will be who I will be.""
> — Mike McHargue.

"The wound is the place the light enters you." — Rumi

ROOM FOR MYSTERY - PART 7

More to Experience and Know

"I will celebrate my weaknesses, for when I'm weak I sense more deeply the mighty power of Christ living in me. So I'm not defeated by my weakness, but delighted!" (2 Cor 12:9 TPT.)

Suffering and challenge shake us out of our (false) state of certainty and security and plunges us into a shaken state of unknowing.

It's in these times more than others that we tend to ask the Divine the hard questions.

Like:
Why?
Where?
What?
When?

Paul said: *"I will celebrate my weaknesses, for when I'm weak I sense more deeply the mighty power of Christ living in me. So I'm not defeated by my weakness, but delighted!"* (2 Cor 12:9 TPT.)

Weakness doesn't mean "sin." It's any moment where

we feel overwhelmed and out of control. It also means vulnerability, and the quiet audacity of being soft and gentle.

Brute strength isn't really strength. Just like pride and thinking you know it all isn't really wisdom. Wisdom knows that it doesn't know, so it lives the questions here and now. Vulnerability knows that showing up and being seen in the truth of who you are is true strength.

God isn't afraid of what you don't know. God welcomes your weakness, your finiteness... it's in those humble places and people that his grace blooms and grows. There's beauty in the broken; it's through the cracks that the light gets in.

Prayer SHOULD open us up to wonder, possibilities, and hope. It engages our faith. Not because we're asking and demanding and petitioning God for "big things" for our "big lives." But because God is wondrously beyond our understanding. And although we experience God and we know God, there will always be more to experience and more to know.

"Faith is a kind of knowing that doesn't need to know and yet doesn't dismiss knowledge either; a kind of knowing that doesn't need to hold everything itself because, at a deeper level, it knows it is being held." (Richard Rohr).

Hold the tension.

"I HAVE LOVED THE STARS TOO FONDLY TO BE FEARFUL OF THE NIGHT."

Sarah Williams

THE GOOD DARK - PART 1
Fear of the Dark

We (spiritual people in general) talk about being a light to the world, a city on a hill... we encourage each other to be the light and to spread the light, and we call God the Light. God lights up the darkness, brings light into our nights, and lights the way. Darkness is something to be dispelled, obliterated and overcome, to make way for light.

So.much.light.

So much so, that we have turned what was always only a metaphor and literary function (juxtaposition), into the demonisation of darkness. Everything that is good and holy and pure is typically labeled light, and everything fearful and evil and wrong is generally called dark. And while the metaphor and the literary function of juxtaposing light and dark can be helpful, it's given us a dualistic notion of two things that were never at odds with each other.

The technical term for being afraid of the dark is Nyctophobia. It comes from the Greek words for fear and night. I don't know many people who weren't scared of the dark as kids, and I know a few who are still nervous about it in adulthood. In the interest of full disclosure, we keep a lamp on in the living room all night long... neither of my children are partial to darkness, and honestly, I'm not a massive fan of it either.

But darkness isn't the problem, our imagination and propensity for fear, is.

We fear what we cannot see. We fear what we cannot be certain of, what we cannot know, what we cannot put to shape and sound and visibility. We think the cure for this fear is to switch the light on, proverbial or otherwise. Light it up, illuminate it, dispelling the darkness.

The only thing is that the writer of Hebrews said that faith is being certain of what we cannot see... (Hebrews 11:1). It seems that faith happens in the dark.

Anne Lamott said: *"hope begins in the dark..." (1.)*

When we are quick to rid our lives of darkness, we rid our lives of the treasure it holds.

Conception happens in the dark of the womb.
Healing begins under the dark covering of a bandage.
Seeds crack open and begin to grow smothered by the darkness of earth.
Gold and gemstones are hued under the pressure of darkness.
Sleep comes fully in the dark of night.
We close our eyes to rest.
We turn the lights down to relax.

There are a stillness and wholeness to be discovered in the dark.

Not to mention that it's not until when we face our own darkness, embrace it and acknowledge it - the things we have labeled evil and unholy - that we find peace, and often the revelation that those things don't make us unholy. They're just part of our story.

The Psalmist (139:7-12) wrote:

"Is there anyplace I can go to avoid your Spirit?
　to be out of your sight?
If I climb to the sky, you're there!
　If I go underground, you're there!
If I flew on morning's wings
　to the far western horizon,
You'd find me in a minute—
　you're already there waiting!
Then I said to myself, "Oh, he even sees me in the dark!
　At night I'm immersed in the light!"

It's a fact: darkness isn't dark to you;
　night and day, darkness and light, they're all the same to you."

It's not that the Divine sees darkness as light, but rather that both dark and light are of the same value. They are to be held equally. One is not to be ignored or preferred over the other. They are just as powerful as each other. And powerful for good.

Besides, for all our labeling of everything evil and unholy in the world 'darkness,' a lot of horrific things happen in broad daylight.

And don't forget that the name "Lucifer" means "light-bearer."

We should not fear the dark, and we should reject the spiritual vocation of Nyctophobia. Let's not make the dark our scapegoat for our need for certainty and constant illumination. When we begin to reclaim our respect for darkness we'll discover that it too, is just as powerful to heal and transform as the light.

THE GOOD DARK - PART 2
No Light Without Darkness

We've made darkness the scapegoat for our fear of the unknown and the uncontrollable. When I was afraid of the dark, it wasn't 'it' that terrified me. My imagination had a field day with everything I couldn't see and couldn't know within it.

In pop culture and religious groups and thriller-horror novels, we use the word "dark" to describe evil and terror. But the evil and terror is really all about what we can't control and what we can't know will happen. I think that's why our certainty obsessed generation is also obsessed with the thriller-horror genre of fiction and movies. For a short space of time, we can explore what it would be like to let go of our need to know.

If only we realized we didn't have to scare ourselves half to death to do so.

Richard Rohr said:

"By and large, what human beings want is resurrection without death, answers without doubt, light without darkness, the conclusion without the process." (2.)

When we live in that kind of denial, we aren't living in the real world that is full of death, doubt, darkness, and process. We quote scriptures like:

"[WE] are being transformed... from glory to glory..." (2 Cor 3:17 NKJV), without realising that you go from glory to glory through the dark.

The Message Bible puts it like this:

"Whenever [we] turn to face God as Moses did, God removes the veil and [here we] are—face-to-face! [We] suddenly recognize that God is a living, personal presence, not a piece of chiseled stone... Nothing between us and God, our faces shining with the brightness of his face. And so we are transfigured much like the Messiah, our lives gradually becoming brighter and more beautiful as God enters our lives and we become like him." 2 Cor 3:17.

We discover this living personal presence most deeply in times of uncertainty. I'm not sure why suffering is the greatest conductor of transformation, but it seems to be so. The reference to the Messiah in the verses is about death and resurrection. You can't have the latter without the former. When we open our lives up to the Divine in the dark times, we find God personally present even in our suffering, in what is unseen and unknown, and we discover that even in those places, nothing can come between the Infinite and us.

In Ancient Hebrew, the word glory comes from the word Kavod, which means heavy. It was used early on in trade deals when talking about the weight and worth of an item. The Ancient Hebrew word Shekinah is also connected to glory, and simply means neighbour: the felt presence of God. We chalk glory up to be this brilliant bright light, when all along, it's the heaviness of relationship and presence. Glory moves in next door and sends cookies over the back fence. Glory is what happens when you embrace the darkness even though you fear it, and you find out that you're not alone.

Glory is what happens when we shed the binary dualistic notion of light and dark, control and uncertainty, and commit to finding the gold in both.

Glory is what happens when we let go and come face to face with the Infinite no matter what surrounds us.

Glory is what happens when we realise that there is no resurrection without death, no answers without doubt, no light without darkness, and no conclusion without process.

It's OK if you're afraid of the dark. God knows I have been and still am. But don't let that fear scapegoat the liminal spaces of your life so you can pacify your lack of control and fear of the known.

Face it. Own it. Enter into it. You'll discover it's much more glorious than what you think.

THE GOOD DARK - PART 3
Seeing Stars

Night and day aren't opposites, they're close friends. They work hand in hand together. They are not at odds with each other, they are in relationship. If there was no night, there'd be no day and vice versa. Both the night and the day play equal roles in ecology and temperature and health and growth. The night isn't something we must endure until the dawn. It plays an important role in the health of our bodies and our planet.

In fact, scientists and medical professionals believe that we are encountering a crisis of too much light. As the world moves into a more 24/7 cycle, we are fast experiencing less and less darkness, which is a problem. We are not sleeping as much, we are not still as much, we are not honoring the circadian rhythms of our bodies or the earth. Our exposure to blue light (which is emitted by the sun, but also by digital devices and LED lights) is worsening our eye health, inhibiting our ability to get a good night's sleep, and keeping us wired for longer than what is needed or recommended.

It's estimated that in the last one hundred years, we have lost on average 2-3 hours sleep a night. Which might not sound like anything too serious, but adequate sleep is crucial to our health and vitality. The amount of conditions and illnesses that are perpetuated and brought on by little sleep is crippling our society and workforce. We used to get up with the sun and go to sleep with the moon. Now, we stay up, and up, and up. And our lives and bodies are paying the price for it.

Without the sun and the moon, nothing would grow. Nothing would be healthy. Nothing would heal. Nothing would rest. If life were all sun, or adversely, all moon, we wouldn't survive. We need the balance, and the tension, of the two. Darkness and light only have meaning in relation to one another.

"Unlike the other acts of creation in Genesis, when God divided light from darkness, he did not call it "good"! At the very beginning of the Bible we are warned that we cannot totally separate light from darkness, or the two have no meaning. Genesis brilliantly names the partial goodness inside which the whole of creation exists (Gen 1:4-5)." (3.)

Everything is a mixture of light and dark. We can't say one is better, or more powerful, than the other, because they both depend on the other to balance the tension.

Ralph Waldo Emerson once famously wrote:

"WHEN THE NIGHT IS DARKEST, THE STARS COME OUT."

Sarah Williams wrote:

"I HAVE LOVED THE STARS TOO FONDLY TO BE FEARFUL OF THE NIGHT."

Our addiction to light is even impacting our ability to see the stars. Take a trip out to the country at night, miles from any major city, and take a look.

God isn't just light. God is night and day. Present in the darkness, as much as in the light. The differing shades revealing a multitude of facets and sides and characters to the Divine. They work together, not against each other. The dark doesn't have to be your enemy. It isn't. It wants to wrap you up in its thick embrace and minister to you. In fact, if you rose above the fear long enough, turned all the lights off, and opened your eyes... who knows what magnificence you'd see.

THE GOOD DARK - PART 4
Conceived in Darkness

"If I say, "Let darkness surround me,
let the light around me be night,"
even darkness like this
is not too dark for you;
rather, night is as clear as day,
darkness and light are the same.
For you fashioned my consciousness,
you knit me together in my mother's womb.
I thank you because I am awesomely made,
wonderfully; your works are wonders —
I know this very well.
My bones were not hidden from you
when I was being made in secret,
intricately woven in the depths of the earth."
— Psalm 139:11-15 (CJB).

You were conceived in the dark. I'm not talking about your parents (TMI), I'm talking about the moment you became "you" physically. It happened in darkness, hidden within blood and tissue and organs and bone.

I love how the Psalmist goes straight from talking about darkness to conception. They are connected. It's often the dark seasons of our lives that conceive new things in our hearts. Think about it. Suffering has a way of conceiving all kinds of things within us. Hope. Change. Plans. Vision. Purpose. Even healing. Depending on what we partner with, if we're not careful or vigilant, it could birth bitterness and resentment in us, too. But that my friend, is entirely up to you.

Darkness and light are the same. It's not that God lights up the darkness and obliterates it, its that darkness is useful and holy and powerful in its own right. And the Divine is in it just as much as in broad daylight.

You never know what is being conceived in you right now as you embrace the darkness you're in. What could it be? Change? Vocation? Purpose? Perhaps forgiveness and understanding? Healing and courage? What is being intricately woven in the depths of your body and spirit as you travel through the dark seasons of life?

"For a star to be born, there is one thing
that must happen: a gaseous nebula must
collapse.
So collapse.
Crumble.
This is not your destruction.
This is your birth."
— Zoe Skylar.

If something as magnificent as you were conceived and woven together in darkness, hidden from light, imagine what could come from the dark you're in.

THE GOOD DARK - PART 5
The Healing Dark

When I was fifteen years old, we moved interstate. It was a week before we were to leave, I was packing up my room, placing things into brown boxes labeled with black sharpie letters. I was sitting on the floor with my legs under me. I went to get up and kicked my feet out when I heard something that sounded like a ball being punctured. Only it wasn't a ball. It was my foot. A steel crochet hook was sticking out of it at an impossible angle. I heard the impact more than felt it, as the metal sunk about an inch deep into my flesh. It was clear I needed to go to emergency and get the hook carefully cut out.

After the anesthesia, the scalpel, and the stitches, my foot's unwanted friend was removed, and the wound was covered with a patch and a bandage.

Physical wounds need to be covered for a time to be healed. When a child grazes their knee, when you cut yourself cooking, after surgery, or an accident... wounds that pierce our skin and make us bleed need to be covered to heal.

Psalm 91 says:
"O you who dwell in the shelter of the Most High and abide in the protection of Shaddai— I say of the Lord, my refuge and stronghold, my God in whom I trust, that He will save you from the fowler's trap, from the destructive plague. He will cover you with His pinions; you will find refuge under His wings; His fidelity is an encircling shield." (v1-4 TJSB).

The root word for the Hebrew word 'Shaddai' is shad, which means "mountain" or "breast." References that tie nurturing breasts to God and God's goodness occur over thirty times in the Hebrew Bible. The Psalmist goes from calling God "Elyon" most high, to Shaddai, bringing God back down to earth, into our every day, ordinary lives, like a mother taking care of her child. The Divine present with us. The first few verses of this Psalm are filled with the feminine imagery of nurturer, healer, protector.

Jesus referenced the Psalm when he said:
"How often I've ached to gather your children, the way a hen gathers her chicks under her wings..." (Matt 23:37).

More than being a picture of military safety, in its original context, these first few verses of Psalm 91 describe God as someone who draws their beloved in close to their chest and holds them tight.

When we feel stuck, or in the dark, or like nothing is happening... or when we feel wounded and compromised and slow; when our hearts are bleeding, and our souls have been pierced, The Divine draws us in like a mother does her child, and covers us in the darkness of a close embrace.

Not every day is for climbing mountains and running through fields. Some days, you need to attend to the wounds in your life. You need to stop and rest and be still. You need to submit yourself to the process of being healed.

What does it mean to be covered by God? What does "under the shadow" of God's wings look like? Is it singing songs? Is it prayer? Is it driving out the darkness with lofty words and loud declarations?

It's more about being honest and aware. Taking responsibility for your life and your wounds. Owning them. And even loving them. Loving yourself enough to wake up and attend to them with grace and compassion.

Sometimes I think it's about recognizing that darkness isn't all evil. Maybe you're here right now, in the dark unknown and liminal, with a proverbial crochet hook sticking out of your foot, wishing you were in light. But you're not. And your foot needs help. And all your wishing isn't going to drive the darkness away. Perhaps there are things for you to learn here. Peace for you to find in the healing dark. Maybe this darkness was always meant to be a refuge, a place for you to be healed of wounds that run deep, and the idea that only light is good.

Not every day is for climbing mountains and running through fields. Some days, you need to attend to the wounds in your life. You need to submit yourself to the process of being healed.

THE GOOD DARK - PART 6
Hard Things are Worth Doing.

Gold doesn't grow on trees. Ruby's don't fall from the sky. You can't grow emeralds in your garden. There is only one way precious stones and metals are formed: in the dark, under the pressure of dirt and earth and stone. Unseen, unheard, unknown.

It sounds like a cliché analogy. And if you've been reading us for some time, you'll know my dislike for clichés and prescriptive Christian jargon. But there is truth to such statements as:

No pressure, no diamond.

In our modern, instant gratification world, it's easy to mistake pressure, and waiting, and challenges, and hardships, as things that are against us. We want to live in the easy breezy light, even the limelight of fame and fortune and reputation, thinking that these places mean success and comfort. We fight the disease, in order to enter into ease, believing that the two are at odds with each other.

Rumi said:

"IF YOU DESIRE HEALING,
LET YOURSELF FALL ILL.
LET YOURSELF FALL ILL."

(Which just means to own what's happening to you.)

Rainer Maria Rilke wrote:

"So you must not be frightened if a sadness rises up before you larger than any you have ever seen; if a restiveness, like light and cloudshadows, passes over your hands and over all you do. You must think that something is happening with you, that life has not forgotten you, that it holds you in its hand; it will not let you fall. Why do you want to shut out of your life any uneasiness, any miseries, or any depressions? For after all, you do not know what work these conditions are doing inside you."

Paul said:

"I have learned to be content regardless of circumstances. I know what it is to be in want, and I know what it is to have enough - in everything and in every way I have learned the secret of being full and being hungry, of having abundance and being in need." (Phil 4:11-13.)

Because contentment doesn't depend on the weather or time of day, on it being light or dark, hard or easy. But on your willingness and ability to live aware, awake, and alive to the Divine in it all.

God doesn't use the darkness to teach us lessons. The dark itself is a beautiful and powerful place of transition and transformation and healing and growth. Hardship isn't bad. It's a necessary part of growing up and learning. We can do hard things, and hard things are worth doing. I wonder what would happen if we embraced the dark earth that sees our potential for diamonds and gold and rubies in us? Rather than wishing we lived perpetually above the surface?

THE GOOD DARK - PART 7
Discovering the Good Dark.

I've spent so much of my life being afraid of the dark. Literally, and figuratively. Afraid of the night and the unknown. Afraid of hard times. I've pursued light and ease and fortune, and every time I was met with darkness, I fought it, struggled it, preached at it, quoted scripture, denied its power…

And missed out on its glory and beauty and gifts each and every time.

A favourite quote of mine by Thomas Merton has changed my life:

"THE CAVE YOU FEAR TO ENTER HOLDS THE TREASURE YOU SEEK."

It is in facing our darkness, entering into it, even embracing it - the covering of bandages for healing; the dark cold pressure of earth that forges gold; the dark place of conception - that we find what we're truly seeking: strength, clarity, meaning, change, purpose, compassion, connection, and more.

"SOMEONE I LOVED ONCE GAVE ME A BOX FULL OF DARKNESS. IT TOOK ME YEARS TO UNDERSTAND THAT THIS TOO, WAS A GIFT."
— *Mary Oliver.*

We're afraid of the dark, but we don't have to be.

The Divine is in the dark just as much as in the light. It's not that God is immune to darkness, but that God works through and in both night and day, dark and light. They need each other, actually. Without one, the other wouldn't exist. They are in a relationship with each other, they are not enemies. In our material world, and in the spiritual, we need both experiences of dark and light to survive and thrive.

Isaiah 45:3:
*"I will give you the treasures of darkness
And hidden riches of secret places,
That you may know that I, the Lord,
Who call you by your name,
Am the God of Israel."*

(The cave you fear to enter holds the treasure you seek… that box of darkness is a gift, too.)

Perhaps you need to spend some time apologising to the dark for taking it for granted. Reclaim a sense of respect and awe for it. Don't blame it for where you are not, and for who you are not. The dark is not our scapegoat for our need for certainty and constant illumination. Practice (and it is a practice) being still in the darkness. Finding contentment and peace. Owning where you are, and submitting yourself to the process of night that gets you to the dawn… knowing that when the day is over, you will once again find yourself if the cool, dark, peaceful night. Like Paul, discover that contentment isn't made of light or dark, but of being where you are right now and savouring the moment, doing the work, and being present in it as God is present, too.

When we begin to reclaim our respect for darkness, we'll discover that it too, is just as powerful to heal and transform and release and nurture and teach and love as the light.

May you, dear friend, discover the good dark.

"THE ONE THING THAT YOU HAVE THAT NOBODY ELSE HAS IS YOU."

Neil Gaiman

WHO DO YOU THINK YOU ARE? - PART 1
The Gift of Imposter Syndrome

It's not who you are that's holding you back. It's who you think you're not.

Not good enough.
Not worthy enough.
Not smart enough.
Not real enough.
Not rich enough.

Not *insert-limiting-belief-of-choice* enough.

What does Maya Angelou, Albert Einstein, Neil Gaiman, Tom Hanks, Ariana Huffinton, Tina Fey, and perhaps you, all have in common?

A voice inside that said they weren't good enough, and that one day, they'd be found out as a fraud and an imposter.

Imposter syndrome is a pattern of behaviour where people doubt their accomplishments and have a persistent, often internalised fear of being exposed as a fraud. All those famous humans listed above, that we might otherwise assume are/were untouched by common fears, all struggled with imposter syndrome.

Maya Angelou:

"I have written 11 books but each time I think 'Uh-oh, they're going to find out now. I've run a game on everybody, and they're going to find me out."

Sheryl Sandberg:

"Every time I was called on in class, I was sure that I was about to embarrass myself. Every time I took a test, I was sure that it had gone badly. And every time I didn't embarrass myself -or even excelled- I believed that I had fooled everyone yet again."

Meryl Streep:

"You think: 'Why would anyone want to see me again in a movie? And I don't know how to act anyway, so why am I doing this?"

Albert Einstein:

"The exaggerated esteem in which my lifework is held makes me very ill at ease. I feel compelled to think of myself as an involuntary swindler."

Imposter syndrome has us thinking:

Who am I to do this, put this work into the world? Who am I that I would assume I have anything significant to offer? Who am I that anyone would/should listen to me?

It also says this:

Who am I that the highest king would welcome me? All Glory To God. It wasn't me, it was God in me. All thanks to Jesus. Jesus did it, not me. It's about God. Less of me, more of Jesus.

Imposter.syndrome.all.the.way.

You are not more holy or closer to God if you abdicate your part and your responsibility in the life you live, the things you achieve, the mark you make, the being and light and love that you are. In some ways, I think people of faith may struggle with imposter syndrome more than most because for many of us, we've been taught not to trust ourselves because the core of who we are is broken and sinful and in desperate need of someone else doing all the work to make us worthy.

Who do you think you are? Because that changes everything.

Sometimes you are not who you think you are, and you are always 100% who you think you are. Life has a way of making us live up to our own expectations. Which is why Imposter Syndrome can be so damaging, heartbreaking and confusing. If you think you are bad, I can tell you that you are not. But at the same time, thinking you're bad will perpetuate a cycle of living that is beneath you.

The good news is, good can come of it. In the end, imposter syndrome can teach you how to stand on your own two feet without needing the praise of others, or a mantelpiece full of awards or trophies to remind you how significant and valid and worthy you are, or even a God who needs to constantly rescue you from yourself (because God is after all, so much more than that).

The gift of imposter syndrome is that you end up figuring that out for yourself.

"Stop acting so small. You are the universe in ecstatic motion." — Rumi

WHO DO YOU THINK YOU ARE? - PART 2
And all the Parts In-Between.

Imposter syndrome says:
You're a fake.

It has you afraid that one day, you'll be found out, exposed, seen for who you really are, and you'll be rejected.

You'd think that it's people who have a problem with authenticity that fear this the most, but it's almost always the other way around. People who consistently show up to their own lives, who put their heart and soul into their work, who practice authenticity and engagement, tend to feel this way the most.

It's a risky thing, being real in a world that values image. You compare, and you are compared. You are criticised for your self and for your work, and these days, that criticism can come from random people on the internet who don't know you, your work, or even what your work takes for you to do, and it oddly hurts just as much, if not more so. For those of us who value authenticity and realness, the fear of being a fake and fraud is as real as the moonlight.

But tell me this, who decides what's real and what's not? Who gets to decide that your work is worthy or not? Who has the power to deem you a fake and a fraud and a phoney?

"You have your way. I have my way. As for the right way, the correct way, and the only way, it does not exist." Said Nietzsche.

The only way that exists is your way. How you express and move and create and 'are' in the world is 'your way.' You give kindness, compassion, justice, community, work, love, play, fun, joy, pain, bliss, heartache, fear, anger, decisions, wisdom - all of it - your own personal flavour.

The only way for you to be a fake is for you to actually fake what you're doing. And I bet you're NOT doing that. I bet that you're taking risks and stepping out in faith. I bet that you're putting your heart out into the world with no guarantees, except the one from you that you'll give what you can, when you can, while you have it. Living by faith often feels like being fake, because there are no guarantees, only guts and determination and conviction and hope and wonder. And my friend, these things are not fake, they are as real as the sunlight.

When imposter syndrome says that you're a fake, tell yourself that you're living by faith. That no one is you, and no one can do what you do, or be who you are. Remind yourself that comparison is the lowest form of encouragement.

Cynthia Bourgeault said:

"One fact that contemporary psychology has made eminently clear to us is that wholeness can come about only if we embrace the whole of ourselves—not only what is highest in us, but the shadow as well. For majesty to grow in us, all must come to the light, both the dark parts of oneself that need healing and the light parts that need birthing."

You may feel like a fake because you are healing and birthing at the same time. You are never just one thing. You are the entirety of life in "ecstatic motion," as Rumi says.

Grace isn't a cover up to hide away all the bits of you that you think are shameful, unseeable, embarrassing and broken. Grace empowers you to be all that you are all at once. "The dark parts that need healing and the light parts that need birthing," and all the parts in-between.

Have the grace to be who you are, and you will light up the world.

WHO DO YOU THINK YOU ARE? - PART 3
Raise Your Voice

Imposter syndrome says:
Your voice doesn't matter.

In the sea of voices that echo across the earth, what is your voice? What difference can you make with your words and your sound? You won't be heard above the roar of the earth; above the intelligence of experts, above the creativity of artists. Your voice next to the confidence of influencers, the fame of celebrities, the wisdom of sages, is but a whisper.

But who are you not to speak?

It's not who you are that holds you back, it's who you think you're not. And whether you can, or you think you can't, you're right.

In this context, I'm not just talking about your physical voice and all the words that you speak, but the entire tone of your life, the sound it makes as you live in the world. It's easy to believe that because the world is so vast and so populated and so vibrant, that your one life and voice hardly makes a difference in the cosmos.

But it does.

Your words matter because you matter. Your words are powerful, especially the ones you choose to attach to your life. The writer of Proverbs said:

"Words kill, words give life; they're either poison or fruit—you choose." (Prov 18:21 MSG.)

Who do you say that you are? It matters more than you know. Your voice matters because nobody else is you. The world (around you and beyond) needs to hear your story. No one sees things like you do, experiences things like you do, or understands things like you do.

Your words matter because even if the whole world doesn't know you, you are the whole world to someone, to the people around you, to your loves and family and friends and co-workers and strangers you meet in random places. Your words hold power no matter how far they travel, because the power is in you saying them, not in how many people hear them.

Your voice matters because words matter, because words are powerful, because "there is no greater burden than bearing an untold story" (Maya Angelou), because you need to give life and energy and language and witness to all that you taste and see and feel and hear even if the only person who listens is God...

Raise your voice.

When imposter syndrome says that your voice doesn't matter, don't bother answering back. Don't waste your words. Join in the endless chorus that echoes throughout humanity witnessing to the glory of God that is your own glory and story; raise your voice with and for others, to add to the beauty, to claim justice, to be heard.

Raise your voice, because your words are building your world, and are adding to the realms of others, so you may as well make them as sound and as true and as holy and as gracious and as powerful as you can.

"THE ONE THING THAT YOU HAVE THAT NOBODY ELSE HAS IS YOU. YOUR VOICE, YOUR MIND, YOUR STORY, YOUR VISION. SO WRITE AND DRAW AND BUILD AND PLAY AND DANCE AND LIVE AS ONLY YOU CAN."
— *Neil Gaiman.*

"There is no greater burden than bearing an untold story"
— Maya Angelou

WHO DO YOU THINK YOU ARE? - PART 4
Enoughness

Imposter syndrome says:
What you have to offer isn't good enough.

It's easy to get intimidated by the amount of good work that's around. Good writing, acting, lawyering, policing, caretaking, doctoring, designing, speaking... There's a lot of good things being made and being done by a lot of good people. And maybe what I'm doing isn't as good. Maybe it's not as eloquent, polished, vibrant, exciting, kind, beautiful, heartfelt, functional, as what they're all doing. So perhaps I should keep it to myself, play it down, hide it, throw it away...

Comparison will kill your flow and joy every single time.

To believe that you are enough is a courageous and gracious act of faith.

Believe that you are enough, and you will find that you are.

But here's the thing:
You don't create and make and achieve and contribute to become 'enough.' Enough is something you already have. Enough is something you already are. Grace is a gift. Righteousness is a state of the heart that is founded in grace. Everything that you are and that you have is a gift. There is nothing to earn or prove. There is only this life that you have been given to live. That's whatever it is you have to offer is about:

Living.

When imposter syndrome tells you that what you have, or who you are isn't good enough, remind yourself that it has never been about being enough anyway.

It's about living with your whole heart.

When you live from a place of being enough, your contribution and expression isn't a grab at significance, but in turn becomes like your enoughness: a gift that is given to whoever will receive it.

You can't control who receives and who doesn't, you can only control your flow of generosity.

So be free, be generous with your life, give it like a gift, and then it won't matter who receives it or not. You don't give to be enough, you give because you have, you are, and you do enough already. Know who you are and know that it is enough. More than enough.

WHO DO YOU THINK YOU ARE? - PART 5
You Belong To Yourself

Imposter syndrome says:
You don't belong here.

I feel this one most strongly. When I think about the things I want to do, and the person I want to be, a niggling fear gnaws in my ear: you don't belong with those people, doing those things, contributing that work. There is no place for you.

It's our biggest fear, right? Thay we don't belong, that there isn't a place for us, with all our weirdness and idiosyncrasies and uniqueness. So we try to make ourselves fit into perceived spaces of belonging by changing the shape of who we are. Which inevitably perpetuates imposter syndrome; the fear of being a fake and being found out.

The world is a weird and wonderful place. There's such a sense that we have to fight and strive for our belonging, for our place in time and history, a seat at the table, an invite to the party. Many of our plans and ideas and hopes, if we are honest with ourselves, become about securing the place we feel we are not in yet, that will make us finally feel like we have a right to take up space. We get caught up in trying to impress and seduce and convince people and wealth and fame and notoriety to belong to us.

But when we live from a place of striving and earning, desperately trying to please in order to belong, our sense of belonging will always hinge on the opinions of others. When we live this way, we literally hand over our power and sense of agency to people who don't necessarily love us, want the best for us, and who ultimately, are desperately trying to fit in themselves - meaning, they don't have your sense of enoughness in mind because they are too busy trying to build a sense of it for themselves.

Psalm 24:1 says: *"God claims the world as God's. Everything and everyone belongs to God!"*

This belonging isn't possessive. It's not that God 'owns' us, that we are God's and not our own. That we live on an inventory or asset list with a value or worth or rank of belonging that rises and falls with our productivity and ability to please.

Nope.

It's that we exist within the inclusive nature of the love of God. We're already there. Nothing to earn, nothing to prove. The Psalm goes on to encourage its readers to "wake up." The only thing we need to do to belong is to believe, see, and wake up to the fact that we already do.

In 1973, in an interview with Bill Moyers, Maya Angelou said:

MAYA ANGELOU: You only are free when you realize you belong no place—you belong every place—no place at all. The price is high. The reward is great...
BILL MOYERS: Do you belong anywhere?
MAYA ANGELOU: I haven't yet.
BILL MOYERS: Do you belong to anyone?
MAYA ANGELOU: More and more... I belong to myself.

When imposter syndrome tells you that you don't belong, you let it know that you "belong no place - every place - no place at all. [You] belong to yourself."

The price is high because you have to take your power back, you have to own who you are and stand in your own truth and believe that it is enough. But the reward is great because you get to take your power back, you get to own who you are and stand in your own truth and believe that it is enough.

When you belong to yourself, fiercely, without hesitation or regret, it doesn't matter what belonging is or isn't offered to you elsewhere. God is already within you, and you already belong.

WHO DO YOU THINK YOU ARE? - PART 6
Welcome Yourself

When imposter syndrome tells you that you're a fake and you'll be found out; that the things you've done are all due to luck and not effort and hard work and your own self getting the job done, you need to have something to back yourself up with:

Evidence of the contrary.

We're good at gathering evidence against ourselves. For some reason that's always been our default setting. "Find everything we can to indict ourselves with and believe that." We collect all the reasons why we don't deserve happiness; all the reasons why the work might not be good enough; all the reasons why we don't qualify for love and belonging; all the reasons why we don't fit in or belong... and pop them into a nice sealed box.

But what about all the reasons we do?

Many people live life like it's a game where you keep score of the fouls and not the actual goals. Of course, we get stuff wrong, of course, some of the great things that happen to us are 'right place, right time, grace and luck' type stuff. But most of the time, the good stuff that happens to you is because:

You worked hard, you put in the effort, you showed up.

It particularly irks me when Christians receive a compliment about something, or congratulations about something, or encouragement about something, and they say: 'It wasn't me, it was all Jesus/God/Spirit/not me.' As if somehow denying our participation in our lives robs God of glory or something.

That's what we do, we participate in our own lives. It's not you or God; it's a 'together and' kind of thing. When you get up in the morning and do all the things that you do, it's YOU who's doing them. Trying to figure out whether it was you or God is like trying to figure out what keeps you alive, your blood or your breath.

Just own it. Own the good things about you, the good things that you do, the good things that you are involved in, the good things that you create.

The best way to navigate imposter syndrome is also the best way to turn it into your super power: gather evidence about yourself that affirms your belonging, worth, and value. Write them down if you have to. Meditate on them. Collect them and put them into a nicer box.

I think part of the reason why we like to say "It was all God" when things go well, is so that we can say "it's all God" when things go bad. It's a way for us to abdicate responsibility, which a lot of Christianity has become about.

You are not a puppet in the hands of an unpredictable God who uses you to do its bidding.

You are a human being, threaded with the Divine, with agency and participatory faculties in your body. You have a heart full of dreams and a head full of ideas. You are good and you do good things. It's not arrogant or selfish to own that, and it doesn't rob God of any special praise either (come on, people). Hang on to who you are and the beauty that you contribute as if your very life depends on it because, at times, it will. What you believe about yourself changes everything. So you may as well believe what is true and good and holy about you.

Imposter syndrome turns out to be a blessing when you use it as a means to build a case FOR you and your life. This is not narcissism. This is you taking what God has given you (your one wild and precious life), taking responsibility for it, and living it full and true and radically. Humility isn't thinking LESS of yourself. Humility is accepting who you are and living into your truest self without pleasing, performing, protecting and proving that you are you and you deserve to be here.

You are not fake. You are not sub-par. You are not left out. Your feelings and experiences are real. You are good work and you do good work. You belong here.

If God welcomes you, who are you not to accept the invitation? Who are you not to welcome yourself?

WHO DO YOU THINK YOU ARE? - PART 7
You Belong Here

Ever had that voice inside your head tell you that you're not good enough? That you don't belong? That you're a fake and a fraud and someday soon, everyone will find you out, and then you'll be expelled, exiled, rejected from the community?

Do you think God struggles with Imposter Syndrome? Do you think God is ever tempted to believe that God is a fake? That God's work doesn't stack up? Do you ever wonder what God thinks when God (if God) looks down upon us and sees the glorious, hideous messes we're in?

Moses asked God who God was, and God responded with:

"I am who I am." (Ex 3:14.)

Imagine if we had the same response to all the people and things and voices that questioned us?

I am who I am.

The ancients used many names to try and capture a title for God and all they believed God was/is. Names like Adonai, JHWH, El Shaddai, Elohim, El Olam... For our Hebrew mothers and fathers, many of their names incorporated the names of God: Daniel, Michael, Elisha, Israel, and Ezekiel are all built around 'El.' Elijah uses both El and JHWH while Adonijah uses both JHWH and Adonai. God is who God is, and God is in you, and somehow our Hebrew mothers and fathers knew this and called each other names to remind them of who they really were/are:

Flesh and blood people filled with Spirit and Divinity.

It's not that you are who God says you are. You are who you both say you are. God can say all the magic words, and yet, if you don't believe them, you'll never experience them. You can't lean on "I am who you say I am..." you must work to get to a place where you say:

I am who I am.

And mean it. And own it. And smile at it.

(I can't help but wonder if we're in the mess we're in because when life asks us "who are you?" we don't know what to answer...)

You are not a fake.
Your voice matters.
What you have to contribute is wanted and valued.
You belong here. Always have. Always will.

When imposter syndrome questions your validity, if you follow it all the way home, it ends up being an ally in your quest to become your true self, love your true self, and be confident in your true self.

And it's all a journey. There is no set and forget. As you experience more and go through different things, the questions will come at you again and again and again. That doesn't mean you've failed or that you haven't done enough. It just means that you are alive and engaged in a world that is alive and engaged. Lean into the questions, you'll learn how to answer them not just with your words, not only with wishes and thoughts and prayers, but with your very life.

Your precious, holy, valid, life.

DROP YOUR NETS - PART 1
Where Change Begins

Jesus had been baptised by none other than the controversial and wild Rabbi and spiritual teacher, John the Baptist, complete with a thundering affirming voice from heaven, to head straight into the desert where he fasted for 40 days and nights and was tempted by the 'Satan,' and then moved to the lakeside village of Capernaum where he began the everyday work of being a good Rabbi.

You know, the usual stuff.

It was there by the lake that he started gathering disciples. First, Simon (Peter) and Andrew, then the brothers John and James. Matthew records that they were fisherman, and that Jesus simply walked up to them and said:

"Come, follow me. I'll make a new kind of fisherman out of you. I'll show you how to catch men and women instead of perch and bass." (4:19-20 MSG.)

Apparently...

"They didn't ask questions, but simply dropped their nets and followed." (4:20 MSG.)

How do you know when the time is right to drop what you're doing to engage in something else?

I write a lot about knowing when to say no, about slowing down and embracing rest, about resisting the never-ending treadmill of productivity for the sake of our commodity driven, capitalistic world. But what about when to say yes? When to drop everything, make a change so drastic to pursue something that catches our hearts alight? How do we know?

It would seem that Simon, Andrew, James, and John knew that this was their moment... they didn't ask questions. They dropped everything. They decided to follow an unfamiliar Rabbi to who-knew-where.

This small tale is preached and written about in challenging ways regarding what we would give up for God... will we be ready when Jesus comes to us? Will we be willing to drop our nets and follow? Become fishers of humanity?

Apart from that last question (we'll circle back to that soon), the first two are a fair enough challenge. Are we ready? Are we willing? Can we let go?

But when you know the story, there's more at play here than four happy fishermen giving up their profitable business to take a risk on a man who'd just moved to town. These guys didn't just move house, or upgrade their cars... they went from being fishermen to a Rabbi's nomadic disciples.

Think about it. When in your life have you been ready to give up everything? Walk away? Start again? When have you been willing to make a change so significant that it changes literally everything? It's not usually in grand moments of opportunity and fortune.

Change is most often sparked by hardship. We get stuck, we get sick, something is taken from us, and we find ourselves not just in a place where we'd say we would give everything for things to be different, but where we actually DO give up everything to midwife the birth of our change.

This is why there is no use being scared of the dark. The crucible is where change begins. It's up to you whether you harden, or whether you determine to say yes, to drop your nets, and pursue the something else that awaits you.

DROP YOUR NETS - PART 2
A Movement of Anybodies

There are two cultural stories at play in Matthew's memoir when he recounts the inauguration of Simon, Andrew, James, and John as Disciples of Jesus.

The first is one of vocation. Matthew wrote that these four men were fishermen. "It was their regular work." (Matthew 4.)

In the Ancient Near East, the most prestigious line of 'work' was being a Rabbi or Spiritual teacher. The Pharisees, Sanhedrin, and Rabbi's were who you went to when things got rough, when you needed a legal issue sorted, when you were seeking justice. They were the elite, esteemed, and enviable. When Jewish kids went to school, around age six, they primarily learned the Torah (first five books of the Hebrew Bible), which was the center of their culture and society. The first stage of their schooling went for about four years, and during this time, they would memorise the Torah: they learned to quote Genesis, Exodus, Leviticus, Numbers, and Deuteronomy, by heart. Yep. At around ten years of age, most kids stopped going to school and would return home to take up the family business or be taken in as apprentice with someone else. Except for the best of the best of the best. They continued on. They made the cut. They passed onto the next level and continued learning.

During the next stage, those kids would memorise the REST of the Hebrew Bible, from Judges to Malachi, and were taught how to wrestle with it. At around age fifteen, some returned home to learn the family trade, or again, went on to be an apprentice of some kind... except for the best of the best of the best. They continued on. They made the cut. They passed on to the next level and continued learning.

During the next stage, students would apply to become a Rabbi's disciple, which went beyond merely learning. To be a disciple was to embody the Rabbi in your own person. That Rabbi's teachings and biblical interpretations (which differed from Rabbi to Rabbi) were called their "yoke." A disciple was to take their Rabbi's yoke upon themselves and make it their own.

When a kid approached a Rabbi, the Rabbi would grill him, make sure he had what it took to be a disciple. Some kids were rejected and told to go back to their family and learn a trade. Only the best of the best of the best were accepted. And you knew you were accepted because the Rabbi would say:

"Come, follow me."

It was like getting the secret password to the Bat Cave. If you heard those words, you had truly "made" it.

Simon and Andrew, James and John were not Rabbi's, or disciples. They hadn't made the cut. They were not the best of the best. They didn't get the password to the Bat Cave. They had missed out. They were fishermen, which was considered to a be lowly profession. You fished if there was nothing else you could do or nowhere else you could go. Fishermen were the bottom of the food chain.

Jesus, a Rabbi, someone who was the best of the best of the best, who held an honourable and respectable title in the community, who was arguably at the top of the food chain, approached these men and said the words denied to them all those years:

"Come, follow me."

In an instant, Jesus flattened the social hierarchy; he bridged the socio-economic and class system divides with those three words. He redefined the entrance codes. These men who were nothing and nobodies suddenly became a part of something and belonged with someone. Jesus created a movement of anybodies where being the best of the best didn't matter.

And that's how you know it's okay for you to say yes.

These men were offered a home. A place to belong. Dignity. Adventure. And perhaps a little danger. And who wouldn't drop their smelly, gut encrusted, fishing nets for a taste of that?

DROP YOUR NETS - PART 3
It's Time to Say Yes

There are two cultural stories at play in Matthew's memoir when he tells the story of how Simon, Andrew, James, and John became the first of Jesus' disciples.

The first was one of vocation. The second, political.

The word politics comes from the Greek word politikos which means "of, for, or relating to citizens." When we think of politics, we think of men and women in suits vying for power. Which is not an untrue side of it. At its heart, though, politics isn't about what happens in old buildings between seemingly important people. It's about how we live together in the world. It's the practice and process of living our lives side-by-side with other people also trying to live their lives, and figuring out how to do it well.

Jesus was born into a politically volatile time. The Hebrew culture and people had endured years of violence and destruction at the hands of the Roman Empire. In some places, they were taxed up to 90% of their income. And don't forget that around 30 years before our four friends became disciples, Herod had ordered the slaughter of every Jewish baby boy under the age of two. They were still allowed to practice Judaism, but they did so with the boot of a violent and sadistic empire at their necks. They were given just enough freedom to stay controllable. The Ancient Hebrews believed that the Messiah would wage war against the Romans and defeat them, drive them from their country and restore their global dignity amongst the nations. When you read the scriptures, it is permeated with political language, stories, hopes, and struggles.

Even though it wasn't in the way expected, Jesus engaged the politics of his time head-on.

Fishing was considered barely above the stature of a begging. There wasn't money or dignity in it, and families would often band together to fish enough to earn enough to pay enough of their taxes and buy enough food to stretch across them all. To be a fisherman was to be at the bottom of the social, economic structure of the Roman Empire. It was a low-

status job with poverty level earnings.

And then things got worse.

In 20CE, Herod wanted to impress Emperor Tiberius, so he decided to build him a grand city in his honour. And the location of this city? The sea of Galilee. Which caused great displacement and upheaval in the local fishing communities. To pay for this city, Herod raised the local fishing taxes.

In Matthew 4, when Jesus was walking along the sea of Galilee asking local fishermen to follow him, he's not on some pleasant stroll amongst carefree villagers. He's purposefully starting his ministry in the midst of an oppressed, displaced, impoverished group of people who were being victimised in a real estate development project for the super elite.

He was making a political statement:

A new kind of Kingdom will be birthed right here; in the margins, with whom no one expected. Not off the back of grand buildings and victorious battles. But with the oppressed and forgotten and used up.

Is it any wonder that Simon, Andrew, James, and John dropped their nets without hesitation?

The invitation was more than just a cushy opportunity to increase their social standing. Jesus was inviting them to protest and subvert the dominant political paradigm of their day by creating a whole new movement: the Kingdom of God.

You'll know it's safe to say yes, not because the path before you is safe if you say it, but because it empowers you to throw off your chains of oppression and injustice, even if society at large doesn't give you permission to do so.

Jesus wasn't a golden-haired man with clean clothes calling a group of successful fishermen into an emblazoned ministry. It was grittier and more potent than that. He went straight to the centre of oppression and judgment, to those whom no one would have given a chance, to the most abused and reduced and belittled people in that world and called them out of slavery into freedom. And he did it again and again and again and built his Kingdom with ones such as those.

That's how you'll know it's time to say yes.

DROP YOUR NETS - PART 4
A Rising Tide

After he'd moved to Capernaum by the Lake of Galilee, Jesus approached four fishermen and said to them:

"Come, follow me. I'll make a new kind of fisherman out of you. I'll show you how to catch men and women instead of perch and bass." They didn't ask questions, but simply dropped their nets and followed." (Matt 4:19-20 MSG.)

How do you know when the time is right to drop what you're doing to engage in something else? When do you know it's time to release your proverbial nets and say yes to a random invitation?

Over the years, people have interpreted this verse to be about becoming a Christian, and subsequently, an evangelist. Being a "fisher of men" has been explained as a metaphor for "catching souls for Jesus."

But if we're going to teach this verse as a metaphor, we have to take it all the way. Are we meant to catch people? Using a hook and line? Maybe some fancy words and excellent productions and events? Anything to get them in the net, right? And as they lie in the net, the air poisoning their lungs and stiffening their bodies making it incapable for them to make a choice, we reel them in? Take them ashore? Kill them? Scale and gut and fillet them? All for the Kingdom of God? There you go, evangelism 1-0-1. But something else is at play in the imagery of the words Jesus used. He wasn't playing a metaphor, but referencing a euphemism.

In his book 'Binding the Strong Man,' Chad Myers said:
"There is perhaps no expression more traditionally misunderstood than Jesus' invitation to these workers to become 'fishers of men' (Mark 1:17). This metaphor, despite the grand old tradition of missionary interpretation, does not refer to the "saving of souls," as if Jesus were conferring upon these men instant evangelist status. Rather, the image is carefully chosen from Jeremiah 16:16, where it is used as a symbol of Yahweh's censure of Israel. Elsewhere the "hooking of fish" is a euphemism for judgment upon the rich (Amos 4:2) and powerful (Ezekiel 29:4). Taking this mandate for his own, Jesus is inviting common folk to join him in his struggle to overturn the existing order of power and privilege." (1.)

It's not that these men were going to catch souls for Jesus. It's that they were going to catch and net a corrupt political and social system and turn it on its head for the good of all. Instead of slaving in an abusive job, held in the grip of Caesar, those who come with Jesus will together call others into a new kind of community. One built on kingdom theology, not imperialism. One where there are no social divides, insiders and outsiders; one built on love and grace, not greed and domination.

In light of that, how do you know when to drop your proverbial net and follow? When the 'following' opens the way for others, too. Much of what calls us to 'follow' in our day and age is the same as it was back then: a system and a way of life that profits from the oppression and domination of others. The way of Jesus will always open up new means of connection and community. It will always challenge our preconceived stereotypes of who's valuable and who's not. And it will disrupt and disturb the notion that some are valuable and some are not.

You'll know it's time to say yes when saying yes levels the playing field. Too many say yes to their own advancement at the expense of others. But imagine a world where the rising tide lifts all the boats.

DROP YOUR NETS - PART 5
An Invitation to Flow

To be a disciple was not to be a pleb watching on as the guru lectured and taught. A disciple was a participant in a Rabbi's teachings, ways, and methods. A disciple engaged the Rabbi's belief system in such a way that it became their own.

Disciples were invited to engage and participate, not to lose themselves, but to find themselves, in their active involvement in their Rabbi's teachings and ways.

In John 15:4-8 (MSG), Jesus said:

"Live in me. Make your home in me just as I do in you. In the same way that a branch can't bear grapes by itself but only by being joined to the vine, you can't bear fruit unless you are joined with me. I am the Vine, you are the branches. When you're joined with me and I with you, the relation intimate and organic, the harvest is sure to be abundant."

Divine participation doesn't replace you, it expands you, brings about a miraculous abundance within you.

Just a few verses later, he said:

"I've loved you the way my Father has loved me. Make yourselves at home in my love."

Episcopal priest and writer Cynthia Bourgeault said:

"While he does indeed claim that "the Father and I are one" (John 10:30)—a statement so blasphemous to Jewish ears that it nearly gets Jesus stoned—he does not see this as an exclusive privilege but as something shared by all human beings. There is no separation between humans and God because of this mutual inter-abiding which expresses the indivisible reality of divine love. We flow into God—and God into us—because it is the nature of love to flow." (2.)

When Jesus said "Come, follow me" to the four potential disciples that day by the lake of Galilee, it was an invitation for participation and empowerment, not conformity and self-denial. Jesus didn't seek to overpower a corrupt empire and way of being and living in the world, with another one. He didn't want to replace one oppressive system with a new, more advanced kind of oppression like some institutions have turned out to be.

We are invited to participate and engage, to enter the flow of love, where God is in us, and we are in God. A place of freedom that doesn't shrink our sense of self, but refines it, expands it, redeems it.

That what those four men would experience from that day on. Simon, Peter, James, and John, were men barely hanging onto themselves, and Jesus came and invited them into a new way of being and believing in the word.

So they dropped their nets and followed.

You'll know it's right for you to drop your proverbial nets because rather than being told what to do, what to say, and who to be, you'll be empowered to participate and engage with your own body, your own words, your own acts, and your own heart. You'll know it's right when the invitation is about flow, not domination.

DROP YOUR NETS - PART 6

Grow and Transcend

Simon, Peter, James, and John, were men barely hanging onto themselves; fishermen, at the bottom of the social and economic hierarchy, with scraps for options, no hope, or energy, to imagine anything different than what they were and what they had. Their nets weren't just tools, they represented their entire way of being and belief system. Every day they tended to their nets... untangled them, fixed them, conditioned them for the work ahead. As they hung onto them, carried them around and used them, they hung onto their lot in life. Fearful that if they let go of what little they had, they would lose even more.

I wonder what your nets are? What are the things you hang onto, that symbolize your identity, that you tend to daily, feed and untangle, and ensure are strong and able to continue supporting your life the way they do?

For some of us, these nets are the oppressions we've suffered, our lot in life, our station, and rank. And although we have complicated relationships with these things, we hang onto them for dear life, because who are we without them?

For some of us, these nets are idolised beliefs... beliefs

about others, about ourselves, about the way the world is and who fits and who doesn't. And even though we say we have faith and we believe, we hold onto these ideas and traditions and biases without challenging them, because who are we without them?

For some of us, these nets are where society has put us, a category we belong inside, a box with the lid on to ensure we never get out. We've tried to open it up, but it's exhausting, soul-crushing work. We dream of the day we are free, and wonder who we would be without the net we are caught in?

In translating this story to our every day, ordinary, miraculous lives, the nets could be anything that keeps us limited and defined and caught up.

But for Simon, Peter, James, and John, Jesus came and invited them into a new way of being and believing in the world. He asked them to "come" and to "follow." No grand promises, no inspiring speech about what they would inherit and who would know their names. No nod towards this day when a bunch of people connected by the internet would read their story and applaud their courage. Just a simple invitation to live beyond the nets that bound them.

So they dropped their nets and followed.

Will you?

Life is a continual shedding of the constructs and concepts that tie us down and choosing to take the opportunities presented to us every day in ordinary and miraculous ways to transcend, expand, and grow.

DROP YOUR NETS - PART 7
An Irrevocable Invitation

Four fishermen woke up one morning not knowing that their lives were about to transform. An opportunity and a choice awaited them that changed their entire lives.

There are two things for us to take away from the story about how Jesus invited his first four disciples to follow him.

The first is that this is a story about justice and dignity in a world where there wasn't much left. Jesus began his "ministry" - the one we preach about in stadiums and on TV's in our brand label clothes after driving to said place in nice cars, from homes that have electricity and running water and food in the fridge - with those who were oppressed, displaced, impoverished; who were being victimised in a real estate development project for the super elite (see Part 3). The Divine Kingdom was birthed in the margins, with whom no one expected. At that moment, Jesus turned the social and economic hierarchy on its head and created a movement of anybody's: anyone willing to drop their nets (proverbial or otherwise) and follow. And he did it again and again and again.

It's not a story about evangelism in the sense of catching souls for Jesus. *"If one's gospel falls mute when facing people who need good news the most— the impoverished, the oppressed, and the broken— then it's no gospel at all,"* says Lisa Sharon Harper. *"Shalom [peace] is what the Kingdom of God smells like. It's what the Kingdom looks like and what Jesus requires of the Kingdom's citizens. It's when everyone has enough. It's when families are healed. It's when shame is renounced and inner freedom is laid hold of. It's when human dignity, bestowed by the image of God in all humanity, is cultivated, protected, and served in families, faith communities, and schools and through public policy. Shalom is when the capacity to lead is recognized in every human being and when nations join together to protect the environment. At its heart, the biblical concept of shalom is about God's vision for the emphatic goodness of all relationships."* (3.)

We have good work to do.

The second take away is this: How do you know when the time is right to drop your nets?

Opportunity isn't as scarce and romantic as our stories make out, even this one about the four fishermen/disciples who dropped their nets and followed... Every day, in ordinary and miraculous ways, we are met with opportunities to change the course of our lives. Sometimes, they are huge and obvious, other times, they are small and seemingly mundane, but time proves the power of small, consistent effort. The opportunity may not have been as evident to Simon, Andrew, James, and John as we interpret the story to be. They wouldn't have known who Jesus was. They weren't there the day he got baptised and the dove and the voice floated down from the heavens. They were busy. They were fishing. They were holding onto their nets.

What made them say yes? I'm not sure. But I do know this: Don't be scared that you'll miss your "come, follow me" moment. It's more than likely that it won't come to you dressed in a suit heralded by angels and bright lights so that you know that you know that you know that 'this is it.' It will come to you in the midst of your brokenness, your heartache, your bias and prejudice, in your challenges and efforts, in your offense and know-it-all attitude, and it will challenge you to grow, expand and transcend. If you miss it the first time. It will come back. It always does.

"You can't miss your boat. It's yours. It stays docked till you're ready..."
— *Glennon Doyle.*

Ask yourself this: Is it ever the wrong time to drop your nets and expand your way of living and being in the world? "Come, follow me," is a perpetual, open-ended, irrevocable, the-doors-unlocked-so-let-yourself-in invitation.

The crucible is where change begins. It's up to you whether you harden, or you determine to say yes, to drop your nets, and pursue the something else that awaits you.

WHAT GOES ON IN YOUR
INNERMOST BEING IS WORTH
ALL YOUR LOVE

Rainer Marie Rilke

THE WAY BACK - PART 1

Return to Peace

Something that is whole is not uniform, or the same. To be whole is to have a sense of unity (not uniformity), flow... congruency.

The word whole in Ancient Hebrew is the word 'shalem'. And yes, it looks a little familiar right?

Shalom is the Ancient Hebrew word for peace. It comes from the word shalem, which means "complete" and signifies welfare of every kind. In our Western culture, we tend to think that peace is the absence of struggle and noise, both metaphorically and literally. Which is a really limited view of it.

Shalom is the unifying of the body, soul, spirit, individually, and collectively. Shalem and shalom are not so much about circumstance, but about flow and connection. It's the harmony that God created the world to exist within: It's peace with yourself, your neighbor, even your enemy, with the earth, and with God. There's a flow to it; movement between it all.

For the writers of our scriptures, heaven wasn't a far off place we go to when we die, but the actualisation of shalom and shalem here and now. "Your Kingdom come, your will be done, on earth as it is in heaven..." (Matt 6:10). Heavenly realms are simply those where shalom and shalem have the run of the house.

Which is lovely to write about, but to live? Come on! A little wishful thinking, right? Complete? Whole? Peace? How are we, in this fragmented world, ever going to experience that.

Through Scripture, this idea of Shalom is not just the goal, it's prophetic. Which is not a word I use lightly (hello baggage from my Pentecostal upbringing). Prophecy is not the ability to foretell the future.

Walter Brueggemann said:

"The task of prophetic ministry is to nurture, nourish, and evoke a consciousness and perception alternative to the consciousness and perception of the dominant culture around us." (1.)

Abraham Heschel put it this way:

"The prophet was an individual who said no to his [or her] society, condemning its habits and assumptions, its complacency, waywardness, and syncretism. [The prophet] was often compelled to proclaim the very opposite of what [his or her] heart expected. [The prophets] fundamental objective was to reconcile [humanity] and God." (2.)

A common greeting in scripture is "peace be with you." It's not really just a nice thing to say; it's prophetic and challenging... it calls us to re-imagine society and each other in light of who we really are, and what we're really called to do.

We cannot acquire wholeness or peace. They are not commodities to be bought and sold, made or manufactured. Instead, we discover them, and they discover us. It turns out that we literally dis-cover them; when we find them, we know that wholeness and peace, shalem and shalom, were there all along. Just as God has been.

Too often we try and fix the fragmented pieces of our communities and such from the outside in, but we've got to take a more holistic approach. The wholeness of a society, family, friendship group, company, or an organization, actually starts in the sense of wholeness in the individuals within it.

We've got to start with reconnecting what's become separate within us; uncover peace and wholeness within us to call it forth beyond us.

We don't have to leave earth and get to heaven to access this peace... we don't have to go somewhere new and be someone different. Instead, we return to peace. We find our way back.

The writer of Thessalonians put it like this:

"May God himself, the God who makes everything holy and whole (shalem/shalom), make you holy and whole, put you together—spirit, soul, and body..." (1 Thess 5:23 MSG.)

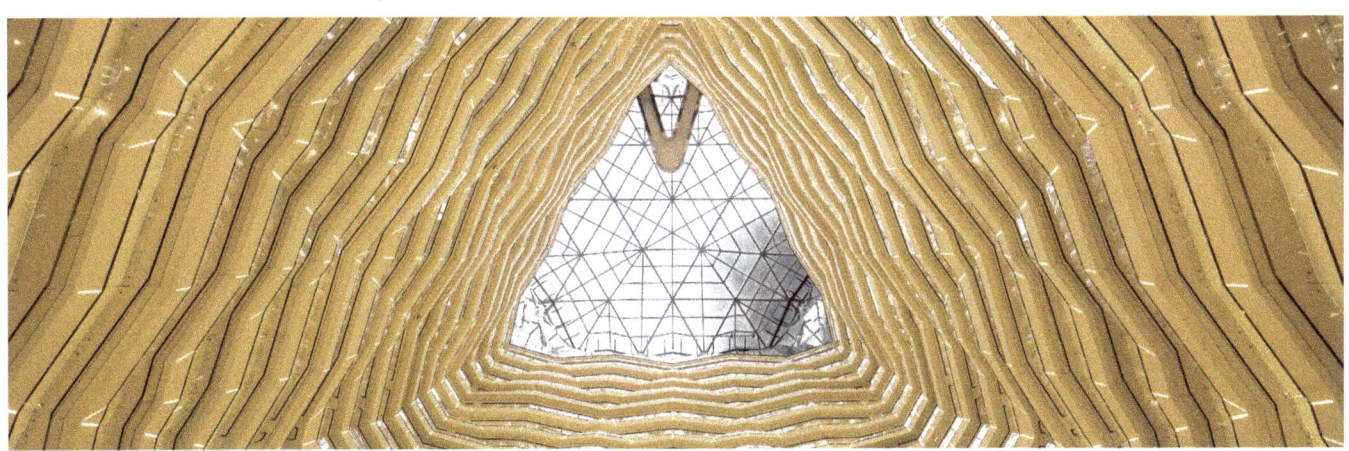

THE WAY BACK - PART 2

A Luminous Expression of Self

Were you a confident kid?

Did you go on wild adventures? Dig your hands into mud and under rocks and into holes without fear? Have fantasies of far-off places doing extraordinary things? Did you sing at the top of your lungs, and dress up in everything and anything and believed you were amazing?

Confidence isn't necessarily boldness... it's definitely not arrogance. It's a quiet trust first and foremost of the self.

Curiosity is what confidence looks like when it gets up in the morning and dresses for work. You may not have been a loud, bombastic, attention-garnering child, but I bet you were a curious one.

The biggest tell of kids and their curiosity are the endless streams of questions that spill out of them Questions come from a sense of wonder and curiosity. My kids are teachable: they want to know and experience things, they want to understand and grow. What I've discovered with their questions is that my answers never shut them up... they just seem to invite more questions.

Adults? We have more trouble with curiosity, wonder, and confidence. We are much less teachable. It seems that most of us have lost something of what we had when we were kids.

I think most of us experience some sense of disconnect between who we ARE and who we are BEING. We fall out of peace with ourselves, we become fragmented, un-confident... we stop asking questions, lose our sense of wonder, our imaginations shrivel, and instead of living from a place of belonging and validity, we try and extract them from the world, people, and things, around us. Thus, falling out of peace with the earth, others, and The Divine.

I was an avid reader and writer when I was a child. I would make up stories, dress up as characters... I'd sit at my mum's old typewriter and press keys for the pure joy of it. This carried over into my teens until it was suggested to me by those in my faith community that making up stories was not a worthy calling. I needed to live in the real world and leave the fantasies behind. And eventually, I did. I came to the belief that the only way for me to be taken seriously was to do serious things.

Fast forward to my early thirties, with a marriage, a mortgage, and two kids, I found myself in a meeting at work.

Now, this was 'meant' to be my dream job. The work I was doing and the people I worked for? It was a dream come true. It should have worked. I should have been at peace, in flow... 'killing it' so to speak.

But I wasn't.

The message I received that day was the same message I'd been listening to for years: You are not enough.

Not long after that meeting, I was standing in front of a mirror unable to recognize the eyes of the woman staring back.

There was such a disconnect between who I was and who I was being. It wasn't a question of salvation... it was a disconnect to wholeness within myself.

Ian Cron said:

"How many times while spying my children play or while gazing up at the moon in a reflective moment have I felt a strange nostalgia for something or someone I lost touch with long ago? Buried in the deepest precincts of being I sense there's a truer, more luminous expression of myself, and that as long as I remain estranged from it I will never fully feel alive or whole." (3.)

There is a way back... to reconnect to the "luminous expression of self" we had as kids. Not to become childish, but to recover the wonder that risks and loves and shouts and sings and writes whatever stories are put in the heart to write.

Jesus said:

"Unless you dramatically change your way of thinking and become teachable, and learn about heaven's kingdom realm with the wide-eyed wonder of a child, you will never be able to enter in." (Matt 18:3 TPT.)

He was talking about shalom (peace) and shalem (wholeness) and how to find your way back.

THE WAY BACK - PART 3

The Economy of Love

Have you ever found yourself in a situation or saying a certain thing, or being part of something, and feel like you're having an out of body experience? Like it isn't you? The dissonance and fragmentation of humanity at large, in our nations and governments and institutions and businesses and communities and families, begins in the hearts of individuals.

We often search for things and people and remedies outside of ourselves to make things right, and bring things back to peace; to the way we think things SHOULD be. But it doesn't start somewhere out there with somebody and something else.

It starts in me and you.

What severs the connection between who you are and who you're being?

In our faith's origin story, the Genesis poem, are two people, Adam and Eve, who enjoyed the run of the most beautiful and luscious garden the universe has ever known. So complete were they in their joy and peace, they had no need to cover their nakedness. When I was a kid, I used to think it was such a scandal that in humanities most whole and holy state, Adam and Eve were nudists.

Until one day.

Things happened, and Adam and Eve suddenly realized they were naked. This realization brought enough shame to cause them to run and hide and cover themselves up before God and each other. (Genesis 3.)

We all have 'Adam and Eve' moments at different times in our lives, where we realise we're naked, and we become ashamed of our skin showing... of our true selves walking around in the world.

We come to a sense of understanding that what we're showing is not fit to be seen. So we hide. The problem is, not all knowledge is true. Some of it is propaganda. Sometimes we run in shame due to assumptions, or due to someones else's misplaced expectations.

When my daughter was three, she fell over in a cupboard and split the top of her cheek open right on the bone. There was a lot of blood and a concussion, so we rushed her to the hospital where they glued the top of her cheek back together. She has a permanent red indented scar, and next to it, a burst capillary. We've never covered up her scar, pretended it's not there. We've had healthy and open discussions about it, and about beauty, and how her scar belongs.

And yet, she came home from school no long after and started asking me how to reduce redness on the face. She's been teased and called ugly by a group of older girls because of her scar.

As she cried in my arms questioning her beauty, desperate to cover up her scar, I couldn't help but marvel at the injustice of false information that we take as fact and then act upon.

How many of us have received messages from friends, family, social media, faith communities, educational institutions, the media, governments, and God knows where else, that has made us feel exposed and naked and ashamed to the point where we hide ourselves away?

We hide in success, too. Money, fame, image, reputation, are good places to hide our un-wholeness. We build false identities, projections of who we think we should be according to what we think others/society/(even)God wants from us... we hide our true selves away and in turn disconnect from our core.

The industrialized, competitive, commodity-driven, capitalist world that we live in would sacrifice your true self for profit and productivity any day of the week...

And we gladly pay the price.

Our culture runs on a currency of shame. The only way to override that system is with an economy of love.

"Always maintain a compassionate stance toward yourself as God does. Self-contempt will never produce lasting, healing change in our lives, only love."
— Ian Morgan Cron.

THE WAY BACK - PART 4
A Return to Who You Are

When we talk about love, we're never usually talking about loving ourselves. We're referencing the love of God, the love we have for our kids or partner or family, or the love we want to feel from other people.

The Church has had a really poor relationship with the self. The self has been branded evil and degenerate, something that deserves hell, but by the grace and love of God, we get heaven instead. We better be thankful and live up to the sacrifice that Jesus made for us.

But Jesus kind of commanded us to love The Divine, others, and, shocker, OURSELVES. He seemed to think that not only are we capable of doing so, but we should, too. When he interacted with people, he was doing the work of calling forth the shalom (peace) and the shalem (wholeness) within them. He made people whole whether or not they said a prayer, quoted a creed, followed him to the grave, or not. He restored their dignity. Key word: restored.

Love is of one piece. The writer of 1 John said it like this:

"Let us continue to love each other since love comes from God. Everyone who loves is born of God and experiences a relationship with God. The person who refuses to love doesn't know the first thing about God, because God is love—so you can't know him if you don't love. This is how God showed his love for us: God sent his only Son into the world so we might live through him... If God loved us like this, we certainly ought to love each other. No one has seen God, ever. But if we love one another, God dwells deeply within us, and his love becomes complete in us—perfect love!" (1 John 4:7-10 MSG.)

There's no such thing as "worldly love" verses "Godly love." Love comes from God. And whoever loves experiences The Divine within their own bodies and lives. Sure, love takes on different forms: romance, parental, friendship, neighborly, sisterly, brotherly... but God is expressed every time we love.

It's love at work in our lives that brings us back to "wholeness, " or as the writer of 1 John said, *"his love becomes complete (shalem) in us."*

To get back to yourself, to rediscover the wonder that you had as a child, the sense of you being fully you and fully alive in the world, you must start with love, and loving yourself.

Jeremiah (1) and the Psalmist (139) wrote that we were known and seen and heard and loved long before we were born. We aren't birthed into this world to become someone that we are not. The journey of our lives is to become our selves fully.

Jesus does not save us from ourselves; he saves us from having to be anyone but our truest and deepest self. That's what being redeemed and restored and renewed means: a return to who we really are.

Barbara Taylor Brown said:

"Salvation is not something that happens only at the end of a person's life. Salvation happens every time someone with a key uses it to open a door he could lock instead."

You'll never be able to hate, or condemn, discipline, spite, work, or prove your way to wholeness. Only love can lead you there. So dear friend, let it bloom within you.

> "Salvation happens every time someone with a key uses it to open a door he could lock instead."
> — Barbara Taylor Brown

THE WAY BACK - PART 5
Come Freely and Boldly

What does it mean to be made holy and whole... kept fit for the coming of Jesus Christ?

More than it meaning becoming perfect and blameless, it's about being made whole in and with yourself.

Frederick Buecher said it like this:

"All his lifelong, wherever Jesus looked he saw the world not in terms simply of its brokenness—a patchwork of light and dark calling forth in us now our light, now our dark—but in terms of the ultimate mystery of God's presence buried in it like a treasure buried in a field. ... To be whole, I believe, is to see the world like that. To see the world like that, as Jesus saw it, is to be whole. And sometimes I believe that even people like you and me see it like that. Sometimes even in the midst of our confused and broken relationships with ourselves, with each other, with God, we catch glimpses of that holiness and wholeness that is not ours by a long shot and yet is part of who we are."

It's a strange concept, returning to your true self. Some feel it's self-indulgent, some think it's new age or too much part of the self-help movement to be real. Some are desperate to be rescued from themselves because they can't see any good in them, or the world, whatsoever. So to suggest that within our heart of hearts, is something good and holy, is absurd.

But being made whole, making peace with yourself, is the tension of holding "something that is not ours by a long shot and yet is part of who we are" with both hands.

Christ in us, the hope of glory... the treasure within, buried, hidden, waiting to be found and unfurled over the course of a lifetime.

I believe that to be made whole is the lifelong practice of showing up; equal parts discovering that we're wearing a mask and dropping it; asking for forgiveness and giving it, too; allowing yourself to be seen and heard and known.

Which we already are. The Divine sees and hears and knows us. God witnesses our lives and hearts. We are intimately known and loved on an uncovered and naked level. And in that sense, we are whole. God is at peace with us and is leading us towards peace with ourselves. Every time we drop our guard, tell the truth, choose compassion, say sorry, accept a sorry, and more, we take one step closer. We recover some of the wonder and curiosity that empowered us as kids, and now, we can marry that child-like wonder with the wisdom of our years.

To be made whole you don't need to be more perfect, successful, wealthy, well rounded, shiny, and better. It starts by believing that the treasure of holiness and wholeness is in us, even if it's buried under all our masks and dirt; it's in the world, too, tucked into gracious corners and luminous places. It starts with honesty and vulnerability. That's what it means to *"come freely and boldly to where love is enthroned..."* (Hebrews 4:16 TPT.)

"...the reason so many of us cannot see the red X that marks the spot is because we are standing on it. The treasure we seek requires no lengthy expedition, no expensive equipment, no superior aptitude or special company. All we lack is the willingness to imagine that we already have everything we need. The only thing missing is our consent to be where we are."
— Barbara Brown Taylor.

THE WAY BACK - PART 6
Palms Up

When Jesus said, "have faith like a child" (Matt 18), he wasn't encouraging people to become simple. Children are anything BUT simple. They are incredibly wise and connected, almost as if they can see and hear things that us adults can't. And then, they can also be frustratingly immature and foolish.

Seth Godin said:

"There's a huge difference between being childlike and being childish. When we embrace joy and look at the world with fresh eyes we're being childlike. When we demand instant gratification and a guarantee that everything will be ok, we're only being childish." (4.)

So many express their faith through the latter... wanting assurances and certainties from the Divine. Heaven, blessing, being right, knowing everything will work out. The greater challenge of faith is to live in a place of openness and wonder and joy. Where we look at the world with hungry and teachable eyes.

I easily get caught up in a cycle of trying to gather certainty for myself, whether it's in jobs or relationships or my community. We work so hard on making sure everything is going to be OK, that we lose our sense of openness and wonder to life.

Life is going to happen to you, whether you're ready for it, predicted it, want it, or not. Things beyond your control are going to impact your life. And things within your control will affect you in ways you could have never imagined. The temptation is to knuckle down, control-freak-it-out until it all irons out, to be utterly adult about it, in which I mean, hunker down, and become rigid, and hide in your success or failures, or a toxic mix of both.

Or... (There's always an or).

You could open yourself up to the experience and to wonder. Make yourself available to whatever it is life has brought you. Surrender. Which isn't giving up and becoming a doormat. Surrendering is the act of presence and teachability. Humility. "Here I am, at this moment, with this stuff, some of it welcome, a lot of it not, but it is here anyway. And so am I."

Sometimes we find ourselves in places we need to get out of. Which is in itself a revelation only made manifest by curiosity and wonder, by asking questions and looking life right in the eyes.

This is what kids are so good at. They're too busy experiencing their experiences, they have no time to hide. Even when they get hurt, they fully give themselves to it, and may do a few times, until they learn what made them hurt and why.

Faith like a child isn't about blindly following and obeying and saying "Yes Sir, God." It's about teachability and humility: openness.

If you want to find your way back to that faith and wonder you had as a child, it starts with opening yourself up to God, the world, to others, and finally (or firstly), yourself. Getting good and honest, unclenching those fists and flattening your hands, palms up.

"Faith points to an initial opening of the heart or mind space from our side... Faith is our small but necessary "yes" to any new change or encounter." Said Richard Rohr. *"Such an opening or re-opening is necessary to help you make fresh starts or break through to new levels. You normally have to let go of the old and go through a stage of unknowing or confusion before you can move to another level of awareness or new capacity. This opening up and letting go is largely what we mean by faith, and it explains why doubt and faith are correlative terms. People of great faith often suffer bouts of great doubt because they continue to grow... Faith is more how to believe than what to believe." (5.)*

THE WAY BACK - PART 7
Finding Love

Kids are curious and wonder-filled and adventurous and seekers and questioners because they know they are loved.

Love gives their confidence buoyancy. It spurs them on to inquisitiveness and discovery. They trust the love they are held within, which doesn't close down their sense of wonder, but opens it right up. There is no fear in love, right?

How do you find the way back to you? To peace? To wonder? To childlike faith?

Open your heart to love.

One of my favourite poets, Rilke, said:

"What goes on in your innermost being is worth all your love, this is what you must work on however you can, and do not waste too much time and too much energy on clarifying your attitude to other people."

Self-love, and knowing that you are loved, is not an arrogant, self-righteous practice to engage. It is about honouring the unique life that is in you, that IS you. Don't waste too much time clarifying your attitude to other people, in the sense of striving and working and proving that you are worthy of love; trying to impress others to gain a feeling of significance.

Wholeness begins within you. The treasure you seek you already have.

And this takes great faith and trust. You must trust that you are loved, you are capable of receiving love, and that you have the capacity to love. You must trust that there is goodness within you. You must trust that it is not your job to manage other people's perceptions of you. You must trust that the only permission you need to exist to your fullest and most glorious self in the world, is your own. You already have God's. You've always had it.

To find yourself is to find love. To find love is to find God. You continually find your way back to yourself as you continually find The Divine.

Paul said it like this:

"I ask him that with both feet planted firmly on love, you'll be able to take in with all followers of Jesus the extravagant dimensions of Christ's love. Reach out and experience the breadth! Test its length! Plumb the depths! Rise to the heights! Live full lives, full in the fullness of God." Eph 3:18 (MSG).

Sometimes we lose our way and we lose ourselves. But it's often in the losing, if we open our hearts, that we truly find. When you see yourself for exactly who you are right in the middle of the mess that you're in, it can be confronting, for sure, but it's also the start of the miracle, the beginning of the journey back home to yourself. Have eyes to see and ears to hear and the presence to be connected to what is really going on, because what is really going on with you, in your innermost being, is worthy of all your love and work and attention. Don't pray the moment away, don't give in to the temptation to push through, don't hold on to cherry picked bible verses offering assurances and certainties that don't really exist. Don't hide in your successes and failures and carry on like nothing is going on. Your life is trying to get your attention, so listen. Open yourself up to the dissonance, because that's where you'll be able to find resonance again.

Sink into the holy moment of being with your true self, and gaze at your lived-in heart the same way God does: with love and compassion and joy.

It's often in a simple moment of honesty about how lost we are, that we begin to find ourselves again. And from there you pick up the pieces, not by works and condemnation and grand acts of faith and holiness. But in the small ways that you pay attention and stay open and live a life devoted to being who really are. It starts any time you're ready, and takes a life time to journey.

And that's how you find your way back. After all, when you're at home with yourself, in yourself, in The Divine, can you ever truly be lost?

REFERENCES

DEVOTION

1). Mary Oliver. Upstream. Pg 8. Penguin Press, 2016.
2). Anne Lamott. Help Thanks Wow. Pg 6. Riverhead Books, 2012.
3). Mary Oliver. House of Light. Pg 60. Beacon Press, 1992.
4). Dallas Willard. The Divine Conspiracy. Pg 64. Harper Collins, 2018.

GET YOUR FIGHT BACK

1). Barbara Brown Taylor. Leaving Church: A Memoir of Faith. Pg 226. Harper Collins, 2012.
2). Barbara Brown Taylor. Leaving Church: A Memoir of Faith. Pg 115. Harper Collins, 2012.
3). Richard Rohr. cac.org/living-word-god-2018-01-17/
4). Barbara Brown Taylor. Experiments with Truth. Pg 46. In Sojourners Nov. 2006.

NOTE TO SELF

1). Richard Rohr. cac.org/trusting-our-bodies-2018-04-03/
2). Under the Skin with Russell Brand. Ep 85. Vulnerability and Power with Brené Brown.
3). Abraham Joshua Heschel. Sabbath. Farrar Straus Giroux, 2005.

ROOM FOR MYSTERY

1). Richard Rohr. cac.org/knowing-not-knowing-2015-01-14/
2). Richard Rohr. cac.org/knowing-not-knowing-2015-01-14/
3). Richard Rohr. Things Hidden. Franciscan Media, 2007.

THE GOOD DARK

1). Anne Lamott. Bird by Bird. Anchor, 1995.
2). Richard Rohr. The Divine Dance: The Trinity and your transformation. Kindle Location 2737. SPCK. Kindle Edition.
3). Richard Rohr. Things Hidden: Scripture as Spirituality. Pg 116. St. Anthony Messenger Press. Kindle Edition.

WHO DO YOU THINK YOU ARE?

1). Joseph Campbell. Reflections on the Art of Living: A Joseph Campbell Companion. Selected and Edited by Diane Osbon. Harper Perennial, 1995.

DROP YOUR NETS

1). Ched Myers. Binding the Strong Man: A Political Reading of Mark's Story of Jesus. Pg 132. Orbis Books, 2008.
2). Cynthia Bourgeault. The Wisdom Jesus: Transforming Heart and Mind. Shambhala, 2008.
3.) Lisa Sharon Harper. The Very Good Gospel: How Everything Wrong Can Be Made Right. Pgs 26-27. The Crown Publishing Group. Kindle Edition.

THE WAY BACK

1). Walter Brueggemann. The Prophetic Imagination. Augsburg Fortress, 2001.
2). Abraham Joshua Heschel. The Prophets. Harper Perennial Modern Classics, 2001.
3). Ian Morgan Cron. The Road Back to You: An Enneagram Journey to Self-Discovery. Inter Varsity Press, 2016.
4). Seth Godin. What To Do When It's Your Turn: (And it's Always Your Turn). The Domino Project, 30 December 2014.
5). Richard Rohr. The Naked Now: Learning to See as the Mystics See. Pgs 116-117. The Crossroad Publishing Company, 2009.

IMAGE CREDITS

All the incredible images throughout this book come from the generous and beautiful artists of unsplash.com (unless mentioned otherwise). Your work is beautiful and kind and generative. Even though some of you may not see this, thank you for bringing such light (and capture of light!) into the world. Your images bring these little reflections to life.

In order of appearance

FRONT AND BACK COVERS:
Eberhard Grossgasteiger

INSIDE COVER:
Frederic Leblanc

LIZ PORTRAIT:
David James Photography aka "Deej"
davidjamesphoto.com.au

DEVOTION:
Dominik Schroder, Markus Spiske, Aaron Burden, Nicolas Schebitz, Kyaw Tun.

GET YOUR FIGHT BACK:
Ruben Bagues, Maxime Lebrun, Natalia Y, Leigh Kendell, Brandon Couch, Justin Luebke, Alex Harvey, Mohamed Nohassi, Olia Nayda, Bryce Evans.

NOTE TO SELF:
Girish Dalvi, Steve Halama, Pedro Sandrini (Pexels.com), Erik Jan Leusink, Geoffrey Arduini, Silas Baisch

ROOM FOR MYSTERY:
Kimon Maritz, Jens Kreuter, Ernesta Vala, Vincent Burkhead, Daniel von Appen, Imani Clovis, Bruno Cervera, Lance Anderson, Stanislav Kondratiev.

THE GOOD DARK:
Cristofer Jeschke, Matthew Henry, Dino Reichmuth, Ray Fragapane, Ananthu Ajayan.

WHO DO YOU THINK YOU ARE?:
Robert Katzki, Alex Blajan, Jason Leung, Sharon McCutcheon, Meric Dagli, Florian Klauer, Meiying Ng, Z Klein,

DROP YOUR NETS:
Karol Stefanski, Alex Iby, Marc Groth, Corey Agopian, Mockaroon.com, Nattu Adnan, Nick Grant,

THE WAY BACK:
Federica Giusti, Tim Mossholder, Denys Nevozhai, Mona Eendra, Jeremy Bishop, Toa Heftiba, Shreyas Malavalli, Marko Blazevic

THANK YOU PAGE:
Richard De Ruijter

NOTES:

THANKYOU

It's been seven years since we first started posting our devotions to instagram, and wow. We never imagined it would lead us here, but we're thrilled it did, and it's all because of you. Thank you. Thank you for reading us on the 'gram, subscribing to our App, and buying our books. Thank you for all the comments and the emails and the DM's and the prayers. Thank you for your friendship, support and investment. We would not be here doing this work if wasn't for the generous room you provide for us to create it. The community and space we have together, and are building with one another, is my favourite.

This work represents the influence and input of many. Thanks always to my partner in all things from family to business, Jesse Milani. If you guys saw how hard he labours for this work to get out, you'd attribute it all to him. Thanks for the belief, babe. Thanks to my mentors who don't know they're my mentors: Liz Gilbert, Glennon Doyle, Jen Hatmaker, Sarah Bessey, Richard Rohr, Sarah Wilson, Russell Brand, Anne Lamott... I'm a better woman because of your work. Thanks always to the ineffable Kelly-Anne, Leeanne, Jessamy, Sarah, Jess, Amanda, Emily, Amy, Mum... I'm surrounded by such a badass company of women who make the world brighter. Love you humans.

And finally, gratitude to the Divine, God, the source of all things, the ground of being, the endlessly knowable one... I'm following you down the rabbit hole with the biggest smile on my face.

Liz xx

www.ingramcontent.com/pod-product-compliance
Lightning Source LLC
Chambersburg PA
CBHW041123020526
44107CB00088B/2995